LANDSCAPING
WITH
WILDFLOWERS

BOOKS BY JIM WILSON

Landscaping with Container Plants
Masters of The Victory Garden
Landscaping with Wildflowers

Landscaping with Wildflowers

AN ENVIRONMENTAL APPROACH TO GARDENING

JIM WILSON

HOUGHTON MIFFLIN COMPANY
Boston / New York

For information about permission to reproduce selections
from this book, write to Permissions, Houghton Mifflin
Company, 215 Park Avenue South, New York, New York 10003.

Library of Congress Cataloging-in-Publication Data

Wilson, James W. (James Wesley), date.
Landscaping with wildflowers: an environmental approach to
gardening/Jim Wilson.
       p.   cm.
Includes index.
ISBN 0-395-56520-0 CLOTH, 0-395-66926-0 pbk.
1. Wild flower gardening.   2. Landscape gardening.   3. Wild flower
gardening — United States.   4. Landscape gardening — United States.
I. Title.
SB439.W545   1992   91-23646
635.9'676 — dc20   CIP

Printed in Italy

NIL 10 9 8 7 6 5 4 3

Book design by Kathleen Westray

TO FRANCES,
MY EDITOR

Contents

Introduction

ENVIRONMENTAL awareness and landscaping with native North American plants have grown hand in hand. In a recent poll, Americans were asked if they considered themselves environmentalists. Seventy-three percent answered yes. While there is no end to the ways in which you can express your concern for environmental quality, from political action to composting and recycling, you can also make a real contribution by growing native plants, including species known to attract, feed, and shelter nonintrusive wildlife.

The national concern for the environment began in the 1930s, when scientists and philosophers with access to reliable statistics became alarmed about the rate at which we were degrading our land, water, and air, and with them the quality of our lives. At the time, only a handful of nurseries and seed companies specialized in plants and seeds of native North American species of trees, shrubs, grasses, ferns, and herbaceous wildflowers, many of which were sent to plant collectors in foreign countries. Now, more than a hundred nurseries do so, and several times that many sell native wildflower seeds and plants as part of their general product line.

Unquestionably, establishing sanctuaries for native plants in the yards of private homes and on commercial property helps to preserve species that might otherwise be lost. But there are other reasons for planting these native wildflowers, grasses, and ferns: they can match the finest cultivated perennials in beauty and surpass them in ruggedness and resistance to insects and diseases.

This book is addressed principally to gardeners who are just beginning to consider wildflowers and to enthusiasts who want to arrange their collections of wild species into graceful landscapes. In the main, it considers native herbaceous wildflowers and the ferns and grasses that grow among them in the wild. (*Herbaceous* means simply that the plant tissue is soft, as compared to the hard tissue of woody plants.) Herbaceous wildflowers are not necessarily more desirable than native trees, shrubs, and vines, but you will find them easier to work into existing landscapes, and they will give you more color more quickly in a given area.

Not many gardeners start with a blank slate, a bare yard ready for landscape plans and plants. The few who do have a marvelous opportunity to design landscapes solely with native plant species. Far more gardeners already have trees, shrubs, and ground covers in place and have to fit wildflowers into the existing arrangement. If you are one of these, this book will make it easier for you to integrate wildflowers into your plantings, to grow flowery meadows, or to create habitats for birds and butterflies on your own grounds. A mature landscape of native plants will set off your home from those surrounded by the cookie-cutter clichés of the plant kingdom. It will look natural, not wild and unkempt — it will appear as if you carved out just enough room for your house, a driveway, and a bit of lawn and left the remainder in woods and blossom-filled fields.

This book will also help you locate catalogue sources of seeds and plants native to your state. It includes lists of recommended species for different regions of the country, which will help you make selections, and down-to-earth advice on how to create habitats in which your wildflowers will grow well and look as if nature had planted them. Then, when you feel ready, you can join the great community of wildflower enthusiasts who share information and their love of living things through membership in local, regional, and national wildflower and nature societies. Time constraints may not permit you to spend a lot of time in the great outdoors, but your wildflower garden can symbolize nature for you, and will equip you to recognize the species when you see them in the wild.

Botanical names, sometimes called Latin binomials, are used throughout this book, usually in combination with the generally accepted common name. If you are going to get into wildflowers, you might as well bite the bullet and begin learning botanical names. Often a common name is shared by two or more species, so the only way scientists and wildflower hobbyists around the world can communicate clearly is by using the internationally accepted botanical names. Use these names when ordering plants and seeds, and print them on your plant labels; they will soon become familiar to you. However, don't let the arcane language of plant nomenclature deter you in the slightest from full enjoyment of landscaping with wildflowers!

―――

Happiness is a warm summer day with mist flower and tropical sage, which is native to South Carolina's low country, blooming all around.

LANDSCAPING
WITH
WILDFLOWERS

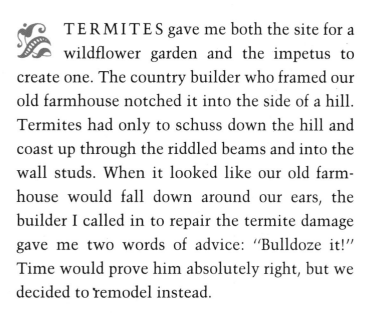

CHAPTER 1

Going Wild

Pink against gray: backlit by the morning sun, seashore mallow stands tall in my summer garden.

TERMITES gave me both the site for a wildflower garden and the impetus to create one. The country builder who framed our old farmhouse notched it into the side of a hill. Termites had only to schuss down the hill and coast up through the riddled beams and into the wall studs. When it looked like our old farmhouse would fall down around our ears, the builder I called in to repair the termite damage gave me two words of advice: "Bulldoze it!" Time would prove him absolutely right, but we decided to remodel instead.

First to come down were the fieldstone walls around three sides of the house. Rock buildings are uncommon in our part of South Carolina, because the uneven chunks of fieldstone are often soft gneiss, brittle quartz, or chunky feldspar. The man who veneered the house with stones had learned his trade in the Civilian Conservation Corps, but his attention must have strayed when it came to making durable mortar and providing strong lintels for doors and windows. The contractor just had to hitch a logging chain to the tractor, hook it behind the walls, and tug. Down they came, leaving a huge pile of stones, Swiss cheese walls, and crushed foundation shrubs.

While the contractors hammered and sawed, John Lee Singleton and I interdicted the termite ski slope by digging a wide trench around the uphill side of the house to keep the soil well away from the wooden walls. John Lee, who is clever with his hands, drives over from Ware Shoals to help me whenever work calls for more skill than strength. I wheelbarrowed the biggest, flattest stones to the trench one at a time, and mixed the mortar while John Lee laid them four high to make a retaining wall.

With the wall in place — fifty feet of it, doglegged at the ell of the house — we smoothed the bottom of the ditch, leveled it with sand, and dry-laid bricks salvaged from the demolition of leaky chimneys held together mostly by accumulations of creosote. The bricks made a walk three feet wide between the foundation of the house and the retaining wall. The excavated soil, when smoothed out, just filled the cavity beyond the wall. Luckily, a twenty-five-foot-high dogwood tree that I had root-pruned two years before and moved with a tractor and chain during the winter proved to be set to just the right depth beyond the wall. It had been growing in the middle of the area to be excavated, only two feet away from the foundation. It took, and bloomed this past spring.

It was April when we finished the wall, and I decided to convert that side of the yard — an area of about seven hundred square feet, in full sun except where shaded by the ell of the house and the dogwood tree — into a perennial wildflower meadow. Bermuda grass and tall fescue, the rough kind of lawn that northerners shake their heads and snigger over, covered much of the area. I plowed it deeply with an old two-bottom plow left over from the farm's cotton-producing days. After three weeks had passed, I plowed it again to bring more roots to the surface and began laboriously turning over the soil with a pitchfork. (I have a spading fork, but pitchforks do a better job of sorting out Bermuda grass roots and fescue crowns from the clay soil.) I purposely chose not to kill the grass with a herbicide.

By now it was the month of May, terribly late for planting in South Carolina, and me with nothing planted. A friend gave me a flat of evening primroses, *Oenothera biennis*, and my wife donated starts from several wildflower plants she had growing in her herb garden: tropical sage, *Salvia coccinea*; black-eyed Susan, *Rudbeckia hirta*; blue star, *Amsonia tabernaemontana*; great blue lobelia, *Lobelia siphilitica*; cardinal-flower, *Lobelia cardinalis*; bee balm, *Monarda didyma*; and Cumberland rosemary, *Conradina verticillata*. She has a good feel for starting flowers from seeds and cuttings.

I didn't bother to have the soil tested, since all previous tests around the farm had indicated very low levels of major and minor nutrients and insignificant amounts of organic matter. I worked in three forty-pound bags of cricket manure from fish-bait farms down in Augusta, Georgia, to give the flowers a bit of nourishment without overstimulating them. Then I built up raised beds by excavating soil from narrow aisles. (Raised beds elevate plants above the level of "trash-mover" rains.) To keep my feet from getting muddy, I spread a layer of river sand over the paths, which later provided an excellent seedbed for volunteer plants.

My few gift plants weren't even a drop in the bucket compared to what I needed, so I started a few more species from seeds sent from the North Carolina Botanical Garden and ordered plants from native

Wildflowers grow larger under garden culture than in the wild. **Penstemon smallii** in my meadow is nearly two feet tall.

plant nurseries such as Woodlanders and Niche Gardens. Finally, to get late-blooming species (may the gods of conservation forgive me), I dug some clumps from plentiful stands on our place and along the country roadsides. That gave me several species of goldenrod, *Solidago* spp.; the naturalized rough-fruited cinquefoil, *Potentilla recta*; common meadow beauty, *Rhexia virginica*; blue-eyed grass, *Sisyrinchium atlanticum*; birdfoot violet, *Viola pedata*; white wild indigo, *Baptisia alba*; white horsemint, *Pycnanthemum incanum*; beard-tongue, *Penstemon digitalis* and *P. smallii*; butterfly weed, *Asclepias tuberosa*; rabbit tobacco or sweet everlasting, *Gnaphalium obtusifolium*; grassleaved liatris, *Liatris tenuifolia*; the com-

mon *Coreopsis lanceolata*; and several species of wild asters.

I rationalized taking a few plants from plentiful stands in the wild by vowing to give away their progeny to friends who visit my garden. I would never take plants of the slow-to-grow and difficult-to-transplant pink lady's-slipper orchid, *Cypripedium acaule*, of *Trillium grandiflorum*, or of any other rare species. In my opinion, taking a few plants from plentiful wild stands for private gardens isn't a black-and-white matter. My farm is growing up in pines, which will soon overrun the sun-

Almost too beautiful to be believed, the pure white *Penstemon digitalis* is always admired by visitors to my garden.

loving wildflowers; some of the wild stands are on power-company rights of way, and that company just disk-plowed the great expanse of beard-tongue that I raided earlier. The roadside flowers grow just back of a closely mowed strip and are endangered by periodic grading and mowing to keep down brush.

Every plant I moved took. It wasn't easy transplanting from the wild during one of the hottest, driest summers on record. What made the difference, I feel, was carefully lifting the most complete root systems possible, wrapping the plants in moist newspapers, planting them the same evening, watering them thoroughly, and covering the transplants with A-frames made of slatted wood, which cast 50 percent shade. I watered the transplants twice daily for two weeks. For a while it appeared that I had lost the butterfly weed, which is notoriously difficult to move, and the white wild indigo, which is a legume and as hard to move as beans. But they hung on; the butterfly weed bloomed for three months, and the white wild indigo bloomed the following May.

I made some mistakes. In fact, the whole project turned into a learning experience, chastening at the worst, but on the positive side tremendously enlightening and satisfying. The most important thing I learned is that trying to design a wildflower garden to look good the first year, especially one that is started late, is a waste of time. In the wild, these flowers grow in fields and meadows without fertil-

izer and watered only by the rain. They won't grow the same way under cultivation, even with just enough water to keep them from wilting permanently. Under cultivation they bloom longer and will often rebloom after you deadhead them or shear them back. They grow larger, and some species tend to flop over when they are deprived of the full hot sun and competing grass, which keep plants small and hold them off the ground.

I did have the foresight to corral my plants of joe-pye weed, *Eupatorium fistulosum*, and mist flower or hardy ageratum, *Eupatorium coelestinum*, in bottomless five-gallon buckets plunged into the soil with an inch of rim protruding. But I underestimated the speed at which a perennial sunflower would spread. Five plants birthed at least one hundred babies, shooting up several feet from the mother plants at the ends of fleshy stolons. As soon as they finished blooming, I moistened the soil deeply around them, worried each stolon out of the ground, and removed what I hope is every scrap of living matter. I couldn't identify the species; for now I have consigned it to the "DYCs," a catchall term familiar to wildflower enthusiasts, who throw up their hands at identifying the many "damn yellow composites" with daisylike flowers that bloom mostly in the summer and fall.

Nature played some tricks on me. Two plants labeled *Helianthus angustifolius* (but more likely *H. salicifolius*) were shoulder-high and forming bloom buds when the lower branches began breaking off at the main stem. I'd come out in the morning and flop! there would be a branch or two lying flat on the ground, held on by a string of tissue. I would snip them off, commenting to myself that the self-pruning actually made the plants look neater. But I never anticipated how thorough the pruning would become. After a mild thunderstorm with moderate winds, I couldn't see the plants from my window and went out to investigate. There they were, broken off at the base, beyond any hope of regrowing or straightening up. What a disappointment! Until the disaster I had tagged these two plants as the most promising wildflowers in the garden, because of the hundreds of bloom buds and the narrow, willowlike foliage. I ordered new plants this spring, and despite their common name, swamp sunflower, I planted them on a dry, sandy ridge to stunt their growth. When they were about a foot high, I nipped out the top of each one's central stem to make them bush out.

The ability of some species to spread by volunteers also surprised me. In August, seedlings of tropical sage began popping up three or four feet from the dozen plants in the garden. I wondered why until I saw goldfinches teetering on the long, whippy stems, bending them down almost to the ground. The industrious little seed-eaters worked their way out until the branches would no longer support their weight, then, with a practiced flip, reversed direction and gleaned their way back.

Two plants that have been outstanding in my garden are foolers. Stiff verbena, *Verbena rigida*, and one of the vervains, *Verbena bonariensis*, are so plentiful on roadsides around here that I had assumed they were natives. Both were introduced to Florida from the tropics, I later found, and have spread over much of the Southeast. Despite its tendency to spread, I would rate the tall purple *V. bonariensis* as one of the best perennials for the Southeast, and perhaps at the top for attracting butterflies. All day long, swallowtails, fritillaries, buckeyes, painted ladies, monarchs, and scores of restless, short-nosed skippers swarm to the ball-shaped flower clusters. The short, sprawling *V. rigida* has leaves as rough as a wood rasp and flowers so purple that "lurid" is a fair description. This is a durable, spreading plant, but butterflies seldom come to its blossoms, perhaps because they grow so low that the resident mockingbird can trap visiting insects against the ground.

Three flowers are probed daily by a ruby-throated hummingbird: the red tropical sage, *Verbena bonariensis*, and the red bee balm. He or she buzzes in at breakfast time and again at the dinner hour, ignoring all the other flowers except for a few geraniums in containers.

This past winter, as I cut back the perennial wildflowers, I moved some plants around to fine-tune the landscape. Mostly I needed to concentrate the species with tiny plants in a special area and to pair more complementary colors. While I can

Verbena rigida has naturalized along southern roadsides and has the potential to become a thug. In my garden it has to be root-pruned.

accept the jumble of colors that occurs in natural meadows, the juxtaposition of lavender-pink beard-tongue and bright yellow sundrops in my meadow bothers me. In future I will order a few spring-blooming species and a few more pink- and blue-flowered kinds to relieve the current dominance of yellow, lavender, and purple shades. I wish I knew more silvery gray native wildflowers than just mealycup sage, *Salvia farinacea.* The ghostlike rabbit tobacco from the fields is as silvery as artemisia, but it doesn't flower until Labor Day and looks shabby after the plants die and dry. Most of the silvery species are cultivated perennials and wouldn't be right for my meadow. A friend recom-

mended the annual silver sunflower from Texas, *Helianthus argophyllus*, but I have yet to try it.

At the end of the first season, I asked myself which wildflowers were my favorites. I settled on one large, one medium, two small, and one tiny. The sunflower-like *Silphium dentatum* grew to four feet and remained compact while displaying dozens of short-stemmed flowers on a neat, sandpaper-rough plant. The whorled-leaf coreopsis, *Coreopsis major*, produced handsome plants, taller, later, and less

branched than the locally common lance-leaved coreopsis, *C. lanceolata*. Its slender plants would probably benefit from close planting. Several low-growing plants of *C. lanceolata* that I dug from a silted-in ditch in front of a country church bloomed from May through the first heavy freeze. The little flowering spurge, *Euphorbia corollata* (= *E. pubentissima*), with clear white bracted flowers, bloomed for months. I know it can irritate the skin and is poisonous to animals if it is gathered with hay, but I am careful with it. The ground-hugging green-and-gold, *Chrysogonum virginianum*, had flowers for seven months straight on tight, furry clumps only five inches high, exposed to the afternoon sun.

Each succeeding year will reveal new favorite wildflowers, I have no doubt. I am reserving opinion on two oddities: *Lysimachia lanceolata* var. *lanceolata*, called whorled loosestrife, and *Oenothera fruticosa*, sundrops. I grew the former in half-shade, and it retaliated by developing slender, floppy plants that needed support. (Perhaps I gave it too much water.) Down in the pasture I found a patch of sundrops in full bloom and brought back two plants for the garden. Although they took, they were shocked into producing only a mat of basal growth for the balance of the season, scattered with atypical short-stemmed, waxy yellow flowers. As I write

Lance-leaved coreopsis is a mainstay of meadows and southern prairies. It reseeds reliably and needs thinning.

this, however, early in the following May, the sundrops have been blooming with no letup for a month, on mounded plants about a foot tall.

I should have foreseen the need to concentrate the tiny plants of the early-blooming species in a special area. Some of the sun-loving spring wildflowers are so small that they were swamped by the later-blooming giants. While I could still find them and before they perished, I transplanted the birdfoot violets, blue-eyed grass, bluets, and spring beauties to the area next to the retaining wall. It looks a bit like a living knickknack shelf, cluttered with my little keepsakes, but I couldn't bear to lose them. They survive among widely spaced larger plants in the wild, but it is dark as night beneath the closely packed plants in my meadow.

My wildflower garden will expand over the years, the good Lord willing and the creek don't rise. In a way, my side yard may have come full circle. When I worked the soil, I found plants of *Eupatorium*, *Helianthus*, and wild violets that were probably brought in from the fields and woods nearly a hundred years ago. Here and there were bulbs of old-timey *Narcissus*, *Lycoris*, and *Crinum*, which is near its northern limit here. Seedling petunias, long since reverted to stringy plants covered with small lavender blossoms, spoke of annual gardens planted years ago from seeds given away as premiums in boxes of oatmeal. A long-stemmed lavender chrysanthemum grew from a piece of root cov-

ered by the front porch slab. I let it grow, pinched it once to make it branch, watered it during droughts, and it gave me hundreds of blooms. An ancient American boxwood, probably older than I am, complicates my landscape planning, but I wouldn't move it for the world. It gives the songbirds a place to hide from a predatory sharp-shinned hawk.

Still young, my wildflower garden looks more like a flower garden than a meadow, but since volunteer seedlings are already coming up in the sandy paths, I should soon feel more comfortable with referring to it as a meadow. I don't know what to say to friends when I take them through it. It isn't neat and tidy, doesn't have flow or coherence, lacks fragrance, contains only one ornamental grass (a dwarf purple species I collected on the roadside), and has no changes in elevation, no water features, and no architectural attractions other than a rustic rock wall and a birdfeeder, now moved elsewhere for the duration of the summer. Yet I like it. Every plant in it means something to me. It draws wildlife like you wouldn't believe — not just songbirds and butterflies but bees, moths, bee moths, wasps, mantids, toads and lizards, chipmunks, harmless snakes, and the occasional marauding hawk. I can look into it from my office, bedroom, and kitchen and down into it from the upstairs. I am enthralled by the passing of the bright baton from one species to another and by the idiosyncrasies of flowers transplanted to less hostile habitats and freed of the tyranny of introduced grasses, Japanese honeysuckle, and kudzu. And I earnestly hope that a few of my wildflowers will be here when, after three or four generations, a twenty-first-century gardener again remodels this house and garden.

Already I know that my new meadow will require less work than an equivalent area of lawn. I did quite a bit of weeding the first season, because it was new ground. This spring I hoed out the winter weeds, spread organic fertilizer, and mulched with sawdust. A few weeds are showing up here and there but are easy to pull out. I carry a long dandelion digger with me as I weed, to dig out the few Bermuda grass roots that escaped my attention last year. From here in, the time required for maintenance should be minimal.

Already I am pleased with the appearance of my meadow as it settles in for the long pull. So many gardens disclose everything at first glance — they are constant, predictable, pat. Not mine. It has mystery, surprise, contradiction, movement, drama. I could never have planned it that way, and I rejoice in its sweetly chaotic spontaneity.

This plant of green-and-gold spreads to cover a circle thirty inches across. The species adapts to sun or light shade.

CHAPTER 2

A Spring Garden in the Woods

Tucked in among the rocks in a Virginia garden, yellow celandine poppy and blue woodland phlox blend with yellow primroses and white violets. This garden receives afternoon shade.

SPRING comes early in the woods near my home. Even before leaf buds begin to push against their scales and spring peepers sing that the water in their ditch has warmed, flowers are blooming through the drab leaf litter. I know it is time to go into the woods when the sun is warm on my back as I am catching up on the last of the dormant pruning. On my first exploration I may find a violet or two, rue-anemones, starry chickweed, and bloodroot. The most fragile and insubstantial flowers seem to bloom first; they melt away at the first hint of summer heat, while those that form a rosette of foliage before the blossoms come along are later.

These earliest flowers will be followed by a succession of others, mostly white or yellow. Few flying insects are stirring early in the year, so the colors could be those that attract the hardier beetles or ants for help in pollination. Blues are rare in my woods; when I glimpse a mass of blue color, I know it has to be *Phlox divaricata*. To be sure, some wild violets are blue, but much of their color is hidden by the leaves. True pink is even rarer, as is red. I have to circle the edges of woods late in the spring to see the vivid colors along the forest margins, in fire pink, *Silene virginica*; Carolina phlox, *P. carolina*; and butterfly weed, *Asclepias tuberosa*. Entirely different plant communities grow where bright sunshine can reach under overhanging branches.

The forest flowers are at their peak in midspring, when foamflower, *Tiarella cordifolia*; the trilliums; trout-lily, *Erythronium americanum*; bellwort, *Uvularia perfoliata*; alumroot, *Heuchera americana*; toothwort, *Dentaria laciniata*; and shooting-star, *Dodecatheon meadia*, begin to shine. Patches of the southern wild ginger called heart-leaf, *Hexastylis arifolia*, having pushed through the leafy overburden, glisten green in moist spots. Toward early summer, the low, furry plants of green-and-gold, *Chrysogonum virginianum*, stud the drier knolls; tall wands of black cohosh, *Cimicifuga racemosa*, move in

the wind, and ferns and mosses begin the summer transformation of the forest floor to shades of green. The woods near my farm aren't rich in wildflowers; I have to walk considerable distances to reach the few patches still remaining after timbering, cotton cropping, overgrazing by cattle and deer, wildfires, drought, and invasion by kudzu and Japanese honeysuckle. Some of the more common wildflowers are everywhere along the way: rat's bane, *Chimaphila maculata*; cranefly orchid, *Tipularia discolor*; downy rattlesnake plantain, *Goodyera pubescens*; and up in the trees, the early-flowering Carolina jessamine, *Gelsemium sempervirens*, and cross vine, *Bignonia capreolata*.

Of all the wildflowers I love — and I sometimes think I love them all — none are more beautiful to me than those that bloom in the woods in the spring. I envy gardeners who can turn even a small piece of their property into a woodland garden. My yard, alas, has virtually no shade. The previous owners planted mostly red cedars, and a tornado took all but two of them. Maybe that was a blessing; wildflowers won't grow beneath red cedars. The old American holly outside my kitchen casts enough shade to protect only a few forest flowers, but the shade beneath a juvenile *Magnolia grandiflora* on the west side of the house is too dense for flowers to grow.

I have planted seedling native trees here and there around the yard — scarlet oak, American hornbeam, beech, American holly, and dogwood — but in my lifetime they will not grow large enough to cast a significant amount of shade. I hope that years from now, another gardener will understand my intentions: I want this grove of trees underplanted with wildflowers!

This chapter, then, is for those of you lucky enough to have a site that can be turned into a garden that will be at its glory in spring and a cool, quiet green place in summer. Many homes have a tree-shaded site just waiting for wildflowers; much of the eastern half of the country was once under dense forest, and despite indiscriminate timbering, building, and bulldozing, some of it still is. Elsewhere, the urge to plant trees for shade or as lawn features has resulted in yards better suited to shade gardening than to growing vegetables and annual flowers.

Most homeowners who have found it impossible to grow pretty lawns under dense shade are converting these problem areas to ground covers. When you need a shade-tolerant ground cover, consider one of the native species. Instead of the ubiquitous Japanese spurge, *Pachysandra terminalis*, plant the Allegheny spurge, *Pachysandra procumbens*, which is evergreen in the South but deciduous in colder areas. Other well-mannered ground covers are the evergreen partridgeberry, *Mitchella repens*; galax, *Galax urceolata* (= *G. aphylla*); if they are closely spaced, the violet wood-sorrel, *Oxalis violacea*; various ferns and mosses; and green-and-gold. In cool climates, Oconee bells, *Shortia gala-*

cifolia, and bunchberry, *Cornus canadensis*, make elegant ground covers.

Some tree-shaded sites need help to make them hospitable to woodland wildflowers. For instance, many housing developments have been built among forests of tall, rather young hardwood trees, densely spaced, with the lowest branches high above the ground. These trees cast what is known as "high shade," not the dense shade of older trees with lower, more spreading branches. If this is what you have, your best bet is to grow shade-tolerant native shrubs and woodland-edge species, because the shade and the leaf litter are not deep enough to protect the small herbaceous spring wildflowers. In my area, native azaleas and rhododendrons and yaupon holly, *Ilex vomitoria*, grow well in such situations but need more water than they would in deeper shade. Don't give up on woodland wildflowers if the area beneath your trees seems too sunny. Some of the spring woodland wildflowers, if given plenty of water, can withstand a lot of sun — foamflower, alumroot, and crested iris, *Iris cristata*, to name a few. Or you can substitute sun-loving wildflowers, such as *Iris verna* for *I. cristata*.

Before you try to plant woodland wildflowers in an area with high shade, spread a mulch of pine bark four to five inches deep in the shadiest part of your woods, then set the plants in pockets of potting soil. In all probability you will need to lay leaky hose to drip-irrigate your wildflowers. Your woodland garden will improve if you regularly haul in dry leaves from piles accumulated by your neighbors. Shred the leaves and spread them beneath your trees — but not too deep, or you'll bury your plants.

Individual lawn trees and street trees are unsatisfactory for protecting wildflowers without special adaptations. They usually cast high shade, and the ground beneath them is often compacted by foot traffic and buffeted by winds. You will need to build up and maintain a generous mulch beneath them — of pulverized pine bark, shredded leaves, or both — and you should keep the grass out with edgings. Use drip or sprinkler irrigation during hot, dry summer weather.

If you live in the Deep South and want to grow pineland wildflowers such as orchids, marsh pinks, lilies, meadow beauties, and gentians, you must have sandy soil and piney woods. Many of these species are adapted to the dense, sandy soil of seasonally wet savannas and will refuse to grow well unless you duplicate their natural habitats. High, dry, sandy, pine-covered southern ridges support a different set of species; sand rosemary, *Ceratiola ericoides*, is typical (but you should be aware that this species has not been successfully transplanted). Throughout the

The cool blue of woodland phlox quiets the strident red of fire pink. A single blossom of American columbine peeks in from the side, while the foliage of twinleaf promises flowers later.

lower South you will find mixed hardwood-pine forests and, on fertile, heavier soil, sizable hardwood trees such as yellow poplar, live oak, beech, holly, bull bay magnolia, and tupelo, all of which produce a deeper duff of decaying leaves than can be found in the infertile hills. Beneath these you can grow local versions (called ecotypes) of many of the same wildflower and fern species that are seen farther north, plus exclusively southern native perennials that are too tender to survive north of hardiness zone 6 (see page 231). These include piriqueta, *Piriqueta caroliniana*; climbing milkweed, *Matelea gonocarpa*; wild petunia, *Ruellia caroliniensis*; the yellow passionflower, *Passiflora lutea*; and elephant-foot, *Elephantopus nudatus*.

———

Merrybells, or bellwort, blooms on the heels of the earliest woodland flowers. Grouped with it are two cultivars of *Dicentra exemia* (wild bleeding-heart).

In the North and Midwest, forests composed chiefly of oaks provide the best habitat for a wide variety of wildflowers. Maple and beech woods are less apt to support numerous wildflower species, because the trees are surface-rooted and their leaves are slow to rot; they pack down more than oak leaves. Some of the best habitats are among scrub oaks on rocky land that is too poor to support a thick stand of grass, or beneath mature oaks on fertile soil, where the branches form a dense canopy. The two situations usually support quite different species of wildflowers.

Starting a Forest-Floor Garden

LANDSCAPING a woodland setting is entirely different from landscaping a sunny area or a spot with sun half the day. Woodlands, even those made up of only a few trees, already have in place many of the elements that you must create in sunny gardens. They have vertical accents, line and flow, seasonal color changes, daily (or hourly) changes of mood, motion, sound (birds and wind), the built-in capacity to create and recycle organic matter, and the blessed benediction of cool shade on hot days.

A woodland garden is a natural alliance of tall trees, lower-growing young trees and shrubs, vines, and herbaceous wildflowers. Before you plant wildflowers, you might want to remove the least attractive young trees, older trees that show signs of disease or serious injury, and alien species. Admitting more light also allows more air to move through, which lessens the chance of foliage diseases.

Next you want to review the number and kinds of understory shrubs you can salvage. Among these, the broad-leaved evergreens — rhododendrons; leucothoes; mountain fetter bush, *Pieris floribunda*; mountain laurel; and, farther south, yaupon; fetter bush, *Agarista populifolius*; and red bay, *Persea borbonia* — are the most desirable. They provide a dark background for displaying wildflowers but don't compete strongly for water and plant nutrients. You may not be able to grow wildflowers beneath or near dense native conifers such as hemlock and spruce, because these trees cast such heavy shade and drop such a deep layer of needles that most wildflowers are loath to thrive beneath their branches. Either thin out closely spaced conifers or plant beyond their driplines.

Often a woodland will have an understory of lanky, unthrifty brush and vines with few redeeming features. Brush, especially weedy alien species, should be dug out, roots and all, not just cut down. If you are allergic to poison ivy, hire someone who is not to dig it out and haul it away. Don't burn it; the smoke is toxic.

If your woodland needs new understory

plants, choose native shrubs and tree-climbing vines not only for bloom but for attractive foliage, interesting winter bark, colorful berries, and nesting sites for birds. Native species are usually more resistant to damage from diseases and insects than exotic cultivars, many of which look too slick and showy anyway. Don't plant just the spring-flowering shrubs. Save room for the summer-blooming plum-leaf azalea of the South, *Rhododendron prunifolium*, or, in colder areas, for hardy native mountain rhododendrons and mountain laurel, shrubs that have colorful berries or beautiful fall foliage, and shrubs (such as witch hazel) that bloom during the winter or very early spring.

Judy Glattstein, who designs, lectures on, and writes about naturalistic landscapes, practices what she preaches on her one-acre garden in Wilton, Connecticut. She stresses that to grow a shaded landscape that immediately strikes viewers as mature and uncontrived, you need appropriate trees and shrubs. Over the years, to her existing dogwood, *Cornus florida*, and hornbeam, *Carpinus virginiana*, she has added several native American trees and shrubs: the fringe tree, *Chionanthus virginicus*; sourwood, *Oxydendrum arboreum*; oak-leaf hydrangea, *Hydrangea quercifolia*; fothergilla, *Fothergilla gardenii*; mountain laurel, *Kalmia latifolia*; and others.

I asked Judy what problems, if any, she had with establishing wildflowers beneath her trees. "Planting is simple," she said, "and the survival rate is good, because the deep-rooted oaks here don't compete strongly for moisture and plant nutrients. My soil is a good loam, naturally high in organic matter. Sand and gravel underlie it, which makes for good drainage. Two reasons my plants survive and thrive are that I maintain a mulch of two to three inches of oak leaves and I add a mixture of compost and some fertilizer to the back-fill soil when planting. I either mix muriate of potash and superphosphate or use 5-10-10 fertilizer. But the most important factor is watering new transplants as often as they need it the first season. After that, they have to survive on snowmelt and rainfall."

The best time to plant understory shrubs is when you are laying out trails for access to the various corners of your woodland. Even if you have only two or three trees, you still need to wind a trail through them. On relatively level land, you can surface your trails with a thin layer of finely crushed stone of an unobtrusive color; this will provide a more secure footing than slippery leaves or mulch. On steeper land, use larger and sharper particles, which will hold against erosion and remain stable underfoot yet pack down enough for easy raking of leaves. Avoid making steps if you can; wheelbarrowing loads up and down them can be dangerous. Trails should be two to three feet wide, wider if you expect many visitors.

You probably won't need a sprinkler

system, but you will need access to water so that you won't have to carry it from the house to water transplants or save drought-threatened flowers. Many areas have suffered a series of droughts that have made it virtually impossible to establish wildflowers beneath trees without supplemental irrigation. When it comes to establishing and growing forest-floor wildflowers and ferns, the total amount of rainfall per year is not nearly as important as its distribution. This is why upland areas of the East that receive only thirty-five to forty inches of precipitation annually can often get by without irrigation: their summers are punctuated by showers. By comparison, even though the southern Piedmont may receive up to fifty-five inches of rain annually, as much as six to ten weeks can pass without rain during the hottest part of the summer. Transplants are hard-pressed to survive without frequent irrigation. Therefore, before you set out wildflowers, run a water line to the most distant part of your woods, following the edge of a trail so you won't forget where it is and damage it by digging. Install a cutoff valve near the house and a bleeder valve at the low point so you can totally drain the system for the winter.

Garden lighting can help you get more hours of enjoyment from the rather brief span of bloom of forest wildflowers. The new generation of safe, simple-to-install, low-voltage garden lights has fixtures that are so natural-looking you hardly know they are there. Lay the wires for outdoor lighting alongside your irrigation pipes to minimize the chance of cutting them. Lights at steep grades and sharp turns can improve garden safety, and special lighting designs can be used to highlight especially attractive plants.

Testing the Soil

IF YOU don't know whether your soil is acid or alkaline, you should get it tested. Here is the procedure: get a bucket and a round-pointed spade. Take soil samples from several places by scraping away the leaf litter and digging holes to spade depth where you have envisioned drifts or clumps of flowers. Take a thin slice of soil down the side of each hole to get a representative sample of the "soil profile." Mix all the slices together unless you find spots that are radically different — deep sand versus clay, for example. In that event, take separate samples and label a marking stake with the soil type to help you select the right species for that particular habitat.

Send your soil samples to your local Cooperative Extension Service. Some states run tests at no charge; others charge a nominal fee. Over much of the South and East, your test results will indicate acid to very acid soil, but forests growing on limestone-based soils in the Midwest or the diabasic rock of the southern Appalachians may be underlain with soil of pH 7.0 or higher. The level of major nutrients

Three views of Judith Glattstein's woodland garden in Connecticut. In early spring, the path is bordered by a double-flowered cultivar of *Sanguinaria canadensis* (bloodroot) and by false lily-of-the-valley.

Later, *Phlox divaricata* (woodland phlox) provides color while a mixed border of wildflowers and cultivars gets ready to perform: Siberian bugloss, wild geranium, and various violets and ferns.

At dogwood time, drifts of pastel shades of *Phlox stolonifera* lead to a rustic bench.

will vary all over the map, depending on the amount of rainfall, the geological strata from which your soil was derived, and its past history of timbering, cropping, and pasturing. Wildflowers don't need a high level of nutrients, and you can satisfy their needs with an application of organic fertilizer at planting time. The tree roots will get most of the food, but not before the wildflowers take what they need.

Applications of agricultural sulfur can drop soil pH levels into the 4.5 to 5.0 range preferred by certain acid-loving herbaceous wildflowers and native shrubs, and peat moss worked into the soil at planting time also helps bring down the pH in the root zone. Although some forest-floor wildflowers need very acid soil, don't assume that all do. Several species and ecotypes have adapted to growing in nearly neutral soils and will refuse to grow well unless you correct the soil acidity with limestone or powdered lime.

Designing the Woodland Garden

NOW, WITH the opened-up trees, shrubs, trails, and perhaps landscape lights and water lines in place, you have the structure or "bones" of your garden pretty well set. It won't remain static; the shrubs and vines will reach up or billow out, but let's hope you anticipated their mature dimensions when you laid out

their spacing and placement. It's time to explore your garden-to-be. Take along marker stakes, a hammer, a marking pen for labeling the stakes, and short lengths of several colors of ribbon. When you get to a place where you want to plant a drift or clump, drive in a stake and tie on a ribbon that approximates the color of the flower. When you've finished, walk the path from end to end and double-check the agreement of colors in adjacent drifts. Most woodland wildflowers have soft colors, but some, such as lilies, are vivid and will shout for attention. Quiet them with white or blue flowers nearby. You will find that interspersing drifts of wildflowers with clumps of broad-leaved evergreens will produce a much more interesting landscape than planting groups of wildflowers with no break in height or texture between them and the lower branches of the trees.

Now you can decide on the species of wildflowers for the drifts and clumps — not individual plants, but colonies of up to a dozen or more plants. If your budget is tight, start with three to five each and increase plants vegetatively by dividing clumps in the fall, or start seeds indoors, or outdoors in a shaded nursery bed. Where it is practical, place the major drifts uphill from the trail. Run them around

Phlox stolonifera (creeping phlox) is available in several colors and thrives in light shade. It grows somewhat taller than the mat-forming *P. subulata* (moss phlox).

boulders or old stumps. Keep it natural. Bury any large, loose boulders deep in the ground so that only one third protrudes.

Don't string necklaces of wildflowers around the bases of trees; that's not the way they grow in the wild. Maybe a plant or two can go to the side of a tree facing the trail, but no more. Don't burn logs, new or old; leave the old ones where they lie and bury the new ones alongside pathways, sinking them partway into the soil and banking around them with leaves to hide the disturbed ground. Wildflowers and ferns love to grow in the humus formed by the decay of logs and stumps. Within two or three years, attractive fungi and other colorful saprophytes will turn the decaying wood into a landscape feature.

Planting the Forest Floor

FERNS ARE part and parcel of forest-floor plantings, and their many textures, shapes, and shades of green make a major contribution to summer landscapes. (A few species are evergreen.) However, some kinds of ferns can be opportunistic. If you see any ferns spreading rapidly by runners or from spores, cut back the clumps and compost the excess. If your soil is too dry to grow ferns well, you may need to build a seep. You can simulate a natural seep by digging a hole, sinking a shallow seven-gallon plastic tub deep enough to hide the rim, and filling it with sand. (First drill two or three small holes in the bottom of the bucket, just enough to allow slow drainage.) Be careful not to mix organic matter into the sand, since it can ferment and prevent anything from growing for a while. Every now and then, trickle some water into the bucket, filling it until the water nears the top. In addition to robust species of ferns, such moisture-loving species as jack-in-the-pulpit, *Arisaema triphyllum*, and lizard's-tail, *Saururus cernuus*, love the extra moisture provided by natural or artificial seeps. When you see wild stands of Virginia bluebells, *Mertensia virginica*; trout-lilies, *Erythronium americanum*; and the southern atamasco lilies, *Zephyranthes atamasco*, they are always in moist, shaded swales or bottomland along streams. These three and many others are not aquatic plants but are never found in dry soils.

Some gardeners have found an easier way than building seeps to satisfy the moisture needs of ferns and orchids that like moist spots. They dig a shallow hole, lay four to six bricks flat and close together in the bottom, put the excavated soil (mixed with peat moss) atop the bricks, set a plant in it, firm the soil, mulch with rotted leaves, and water the plant frequently until it is well established. The roots grow around and between the bricks to reach the moisture that accumulates beneath them. You've seen lines of plants flourishing where blacktop or concrete surfaces meet the soil; this is because they send roots under the pavement to reach the trapped water. The same principle applies to bricks and stones buried in forest soil.

Gardeners with large areas of sloping woodlands often find it useful to build terraces with logs that will eventually decay. Lay the logs across the slope, rake away the leaves, fill in behind the logs with finely ground pine or hardwood bark, and transplant wildflowers, mosses, and ferns into planting pockets filled with potting soil. Then lay leaky hose for drip irrigation and rake leaves over the hose to hide it. A few fern species — ebony spleenwort, *Asplenium platyneuron*, and Christmas fern, *Polystichum acrostichoides*, for example — can take fairly dry soil after setting a good root system. Maidenhair ferns, *Adiantum pedatum*, are almost as tolerant. However, the richest variety of ferns is found in the cool, moist forests of the North, in the southern mountains, and in the Pacific Northwest, where snowmelt keeps the soil moist until late spring, after which periodic summer showers supply the consistent moisture preferred by vigorous species. At lower, warmer elevations, wild ferns and moisture-loving wildflowers tend to concentrate on eastern and northern slopes that are protected from the afternoon sun. Further, they can be found in greater numbers near the bottom of slopes, where moisture from higher elevations seeps out.

The techniques of planting in a woodland garden are very different from those for a sunny field or a cultivated border. Never run a power tiller beneath trees. You can wear out the tiller and damage the trees' feeder roots, most of which are in the top eight inches of soil. Instead, use a mattock to take out clumps of grass, sedge, and brush and to loosen compacted soil. Dig only where you intend to set out plants of wildflowers. If you hit a sizable root, move over and dig in an open spot. Most woodland species, with the exception of those that like boggy conditions, prefer well-aerated, rather loose soil. If you have composted leaves, run them through a shredder and mix them half and half with the soil taken from planting holes. Also, mix in about 10 percent moistened sphagnum peat moss by volume and about one cup of organic fertilizer such as cottonseed meal, soybean meal, or blood meal for each plant. Rake undecomposed leaves away from the planting area; dry, intact leaves can interfere with the passage of water through the enriched soil around transplants. Dig a hole about one and a half feet across and one foot deep for each transplant and chop out all the competing tree roots, which can dry out the soil and hurt your wildflowers.

Ideally, all your preparations should be completed and plants ordered by late summer. Fall is the best time for transplanting spring wildflowers, except in parts of hardiness zone 5 and north where snow cover is sparse. (A hardiness zone map is included on page 231.) Wait until most of the leaves have dropped, then rake them away from your planting sites. Turn under the composted leaves, mix in fertilizer and sulfur (if needed), make planting holes, and set the plants in place. Water thoroughly every day or so for a week, and weekly thereafter until and if the soil freezes. In the South, you should water new transplants during winter dry spells.

Buy or rent a leaf shredder, chop the fallen leaves, and use them to mulch between the plants. If you don't have a shredder, run a rotary lawn mower over a pile of leaves to shred them. Shredded leaves don't blow around or pack down when wet, and they absorb water more readily and decompose faster than intact leaves. By shredding leaves, you can reduce their volume by as much as 50 percent — not a small consideration where large trees are involved.

How much leaf raking you have to do depends on the size of your woods and its dominant tree species. Maple and beech leaves are slow to decay and tend to mat down. Oak leaves decay somewhat faster but accumulate to such a depth that they may need raking. If you have only a small patch of woods, raking is no big chore. Raking during the fall is not so vital in pine or mixed pine-hardwood forests, where the pine straw keeps leaves from packing down. You can wait until spring, but raking around the tender shoots of wildflowers requires a light touch.

Never burn or haul away excess leaves; compost them. You can use them to main-tain the leaf mold necessary to grow forest-floor flowers; in their decay, leaves return nutrients to the soil. If your neighbors bag leaves to be picked up for dumping, ask if you can take them, then shred and compost them to build up the leaf mold in your soil. This is especially important in the South and areas of the West where high prevailing soil temperatures decompose leaf litter rapidly and allow only a thin duff to form beneath trees.

Just as important as raking leaves is watching your plants for signs of drought. The first spring after fall planting is the hardest on new plants, because they have to compete with tree roots when their own root systems are less than fully developed (hence the value of clearing all tree roots out of the planting holes). Late summer droughts — three weeks or more without rain — can also hurt wildflowers. In general, spot-watering groups of plants works better and is less wasteful than sprinkling. Attach a "water breaker" bubbler to your hose to eliminate damage from water blast. However, you may soon wish to install the best of all systems for watering — drip irrigation. With a drip system in place, you won't have to drag hoses around your property and run the risk of damaging plants. In the West, sprinkler irrigation or frequent watering of any sort under oak trees is never advisable, since it can trigger an outbreak of armillaria root rot, which can severely injure or damage trees and surrounding ornamentals.

Growing Wildflowers Beneath Difficult Trees

IT'S RELATIVELY easy to make a woodland garden under eastern and midwestern deciduous species such as oak, hickory, ash, black gum, cherry, and birch, perhaps mixed with a few pines. These species don't compete as strongly with wildflowers as some surface-rooted tree species. Here's how to grow wildflowers under difficult maple, beech, and sweet gum trees, and shallow-rooted water oaks in the South.

First, if you can do it without ruining their looks, limb up the trees to admit more light. Next, mow the grass beneath them as short as you can with your mower. To keep tree roots out of the root zone of your wildflowers, lay down porous spun-fiber landscape cloth (not sheet plastic) with the edges overlapped six inches. Two layers of landscape cloth will foil tree roots even longer. Over the cloth spread three to five (no more) inches of pine or

The pure white blossoms of *Dicentra exemia* var. 'Alba' show up against the drab leaf litter on the forest floor.

Green against green: immaculately groomed moss makes an ideal foil for darker green native rhododendrons and leucothoes.

hardwood bark mulch, but keep it two feet away from the bole of each tree. Make pockets in the mulch and fill them with potting soil, but don't puncture the landscape cloth. Then set in your plants.

You will need to water fairly often until the wildflowers are established, but it is a small price to pay for converting the barren trouble spot under lawn trees into a wildflower garden. Water and oxygen will percolate through the fibrous mulch, and gases can escape. If the trees are healthy, the overburden of mulch should cause no problem, which is not the case when you cover roots with a deep layer of soil. (You would not, however, want to risk deep-mulching a tree growing in a low spot where water tends to accumulate.) After two or three years you may discover that an occasional tree root has penetrated the layer of landscape fabric to forage in the mulch. Trace it back to the point of entry by tugging gently, then prune it off. The only problem with landscape cloth comes when and if you have to remove it: the fabric can become so matted with plant roots that you have to clip roots as you peel it back, a tedious and difficult job.

Selecting the Wildflowers

YOU WILL always be safe growing the flowers that are native to your own area, but most of us don't want to be limited by geography. (And we enjoy a challenge!) Some of the eastern forest-floor wild-flower species can be found from Minnesota and Maine to extreme northern Florida and east Texas, and will adapt from one climatic extreme to the other. (Some, but not all — certain species have developed ecotypes to survive in demanding sites, and these grow best when planted near home.) Several of the southern mountain forest wildflowers will adapt to northern climates, and lowland northwestern species to the upper South. Ordinarily, however, mountain woodland species that are accustomed to a cool, rainy climate will not grow well in the heat and dry soil of lowland gardens. Coastal California forest wildflowers don't travel well; accustomed to definite wet-dry cycles and relatively moderate winters, they are rarely happy in other climates.

There are advantages to ordering indigenous species from nurseries within a hundred miles of your home, but most wildflower enthusiasts soon hurdle this barrier and patronize nurseries that offer the species that intrigue them. Although a few popular species are sold at retail nurseries, the widest selection comes from mail-order specialists. Whichever nursery you choose, read its catalogue carefully for the notice "Our wildflower plants are propagated and grown at this nursery." Don't be taken in by the sometimes deliberately deceptive term "nursery grown," which can be bent to cover plants that are collected in the wild and grown to a larger size in the nursery. The majority of species that don't transplant well or that require many years to reach bloom size are forest types, including pink lady's-slipper, *Cypripedium acaule*; Oconee bells, *Shortia galacifolia*; large-flowered trillium, *Trillium grandiflorum*; and painted trillium, *T. undulatum*. Question retailers carefully about the source of their woodland or bog wildflowers. In 1990, for example, five people were apprehended while removing buckets of Venus's-flytrap from protected lands. They confessed to planning to sell them to a nursery. That's as reprehensible as stealing the president's limousine and taking it to a chop shop! Furthermore, Venus's-flytrap plants usually perish shortly after being removed from their swampy peat-bog habitat.

To match plants and habitat, you have to think like a plant. Although you have a great deal of latitude, you tempt fate when you place a plant in an environment drastically different from its native niche. Look up and down and all around, dig in the soil, and if all your senses tell you that the wildflower you have chosen should be happy there, go ahead and plant it. Virtually every time, if the soil is well drained and well aerated with organic matter, the plant will grow and thrive. One word of caution: if you want to grow a species that has adapted to dry, sandy soil, you will probably have to haul in a load of

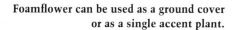

Foamflower can be used as a ground cover or as a single accent plant.

sand; these species are finicky and will sulk and eventually die in clay woodland soil.

Now that plant breeders are beginning to select wildflowers for more color and special blossom characteristics, you will often find choice selections of wild species displayed with the named cultivars of shade-loving perennials. Gradually the line is blurring between what we know as "wildflowers" and what the trade sells as "perennials." You have to make up your mind about whether to grow the plain, unvarnished wild species or hybrids or selections that have been improved by breeders and given cultivar names. Many of the named cultivars are simply color breaks — the white woodland phlox, for instance, has been selected from a species that in the wild is blue, and double-flowered cultivars come from normally single-flowered species. To me, the cultivars selected from native species for different colors or slightly larger blossoms are entirely acceptable in a wildflower garden, but most flowers with double blossoms are so obviously man-modified that they jar my sensibilities.

To save money and have the satisfaction of growing your own plants, you can start with seeds. Either buy them or collect them yourself from plants marked with colored tape when they are in flower. If you don't want to trek into the woods, ask around. Fellow wildflower enthusiasts are usually willing to share or swap seeds. If you want rare or unusual species, order

from seed exchanges at botanical gardens. Except for the species that grow slowly, most woodland wildflowers will bloom a year or two after you start the seeds. The trilliums and orchids are slow; some can require as much as seven years to reach the flowering stage. At the other extreme, avoid wildflowers or perennials that tend to take over: may-apple, *Podophyllum peltatum*; bracken fern; violet species that form large, leafy clumps, like the common wild violet, *Viola sororia*; and such exotics as European or Italian arum, *Arum italicum*, and European ginger, *Asarum europaeum*. Once you get clumps of certain wildflowers established, you will be amazed at the number of seedlings that will grow from dropped seeds. I have seen the greatest concentration of seedlings around plants surrounded by moss or growing next to a patch mulched with bark or gravel. Leaf litter apparently isn't the greatest place for tiny seeds to drop and germinate.

Extending the Season

IT IS the nature of the forest-floor garden to bloom in spring, before trees leaf out fully, but you can extend the season with later-blooming native species such as spotted wintergreen, *Chimaphila maculata*; black cohosh, *Cimicifuga racemosa*; white snakeroot, *Eupatorium rugosum*; or cultivars such as *Heuchera* 'Palace Purple'. It's worth the effort, for you might gain an extra month or so of color. Still, most gardeners cheerfully settle for a gradual shift from spring and early summer color into the cool green of shrubs, ground covers, ferns, and mosses. Later, the fall and winter berries brighten the landscape in earthbound auroras; in our area the light purple *Callicarpa* we refer to as "French mulberry" is especially vivid. Wildflowers have to dance to the rhythm of the forest, and after a brief spring fling, most fade into the landscape with the closing over of the woodland canopy.

The exotic *Anemone blanda* 'White Splendor' sets off the native whippoorwill-flower in a New England woodland garden.

CHAPTER 3

Meadows

This is why flowery meadows are so popular — they provide a delightful array of flower colors and forms from early summer through fall frost, with later kinds taking up the pace as early-flowering annuals fade.

I CAN'T remember when a landscape style so captured the American gardener as the meadow has today. Perhaps we are tired of designer gardens and highly bred flowers that are ever brighter, shorter, showier, and more uniform. Perhaps as open fields shrink or are rimmed by NO TRESPASSING signs, we feel compelled to create little pieces of country for ourselves. Perhaps it is because of concern for the environment and our natural resources. The typical suburban landscape, and especially turf grass, is a heavy consumer of fertilizers, insecticides, and weedkillers, which can run off or percolate into our water supply. Lawns are the biggest domestic consumer of water, to say nothing of energy (our own and that which powers our mowers).

And perhaps it is the sum of these things plus the romantic in each of us.

In the idyllic world of the catalogue copywriter, all you have to do to create a beautiful meadow is sprinkle a canful of seeds over a piece of land, sit back, and wait for it to bloom. Year after year the perennial flowers will return and crowd out the weeds; each fall, when the annuals have finished their bloom, they will generously reseed themselves to come back another year.

It's a beautiful fantasy, but that's all it is — a fantasy. If you've tried to make a meadow this way and given up in disgust, please try again. The fact is that you can grow a beautiful meadow, but you have to know how to do it and what to expect.

Meadows: What's in a Name

YOU WON'T be far off the mark if you divide meadows into two types: annual and perennial. Annual meadows are basically what you get when you plant packaged seed mixtures. A few perennials, many of them rather weedy garden flowers that naturalize readily, may persist. Perennial meadows, however, are what you get when you set out plants of perennial wildflower species native to your area.

Serious wildflower enthusiasts, myself included, cringe when we see the term "wildflower meadows" used to describe what grows from most packaged seed mixtures. It is a misnomer. The packagers of the seed mixtures know that customers want lots of bright colors right away, and that they want variety, flowery surprises, and mystery flowers. That's what they get, but partly in the form of garden flowers, not wildflowers native to their area, or even native to this country. (For an analysis of popular seed mixtures, see Appendix I.) And many of the native annuals in meadow seed mixtures are originally from the West Coast, the dry Southwest, the Rockies, and dry upland areas of Mexico. Although they will reseed themselves in their native habitats, don't expect them to come back reliably in other parts of the country.

Read the analysis label on the package. If the mixture contains perennials as well as annuals, you should guard against aggressive, weedy species. I have seen meadows where the kind of yarrow called milfoil, *Achillea millefolium*, grew into a dense mat that excluded almost all other flowers, or where dame's rocket, *Hesperis matronalis*; Queen Anne's lace, *Daucus carota*; and the primitive ox-eye form of Shasta daisies, *Chrysanthemum leucanthemum*, took over after the third year. Desirable native perennial wildflowers usually get off to a slow start and can be swamped by these opportunistic aliens.

Just as these mixtures are not truly

wildflower mixes, neither are they authentic meadow mixes. In the East and South (other than east Texas), natural meadows are small and have just a few species of wildflowers, which grow in patches or drifts, mingled with native grasses. In the West and Southwest, meadows are more like huge fields, blanketed with seasonal shows of single species or at the most with patches of two or three species mixed with native grasses. When you stand back and look at natural meadows, eastern or western, your eye accepts the high proportion of grasses to flowers as appropriate to a wild situation.

But let's not spoil the fun of meadow gardening by insisting that man-made meadows have to be authentic. If you like lots of color and want it quickly, why not plant the idealized version? To lessen the confusion, let's call these "flowery meadows" or "cultivated meadows" or, my preference, "annual meadows." And let's not plant the packaged seed mixtures where the plants or seeds could escape into nearby agricultural fields or wild land and become pests.

Sturdy native flowers such as butterfly weed, New England aster, and purple prairie coneflower have helped this Tennessee meadow endure for several years.

Regardless of the name you give to your bright but short-lived meadow, you will get the best results from a high-quality seed mixture packed for your geographical region. You should get brilliant color from a dozen or so species the first year, and blooms all season long as later species succeed the early bloomers. But let me caution you about unrealistic expectations for the second and succeeding years. Only the hardy perennials and a few reseeding annuals will come back. For this reason, many gardeners fortify their annual meadows by overseeding each fall or spring, or turn over the soil to a shallow

Spotted bee balm makes a robust, colorful plant for sunny, moist meadows.

depth and plant new seeds each year, or plug in plants of native perennials to gain permanence.

If you live in the East or South and want a long-lived meadow that requires less labor, plant it with perennial species native to your part of your state. Use wildflowers alone if you want it pretty; add native grasses if you want it authentic. Your meadow will start slowly. It won't be flashy, but it will look as if it grew nat-

urally, and it will do a great job of attracting birds and butterflies.

Perennial meadows are to the East and South what prairies are to the Midwest and Great Plains. In the wild, they are found in clearings in forests or on land too rocky or infertile to support a thick stand of mat-forming grass. Perennial meadows come back year after year. Man-made versions are like large, sun-drenched beds and borders of cultivated perennials, except that they are planted informally with native wildflowers and grasses. They appeal to wildflower enthusiasts who want more natural-looking, longer-lived mead-

Many species of *Liatris* (blazing star or gayfeather) adorn natural meadows from the Great Plains east to the Atlantic Coast and south through Texas. They are one of the finest, most adaptable native plants for perennial meadows.

ows than they can grow from flower seed mixtures packaged for annual meadows. The wildflower garden I am growing in my side yard could be called a perennial meadow.

If you plant a perennial meadow with species that are native to within a hundred or so miles of your garden, you can still have plenty of variety. Most gardeners, however, receive catalogues from all over their geographic region and soon reach out for well-adapted species from some distance away. (Professional botanists hate to see this happen, because it can conceivably destroy the distinctiveness of local ecotypes — small colonies of species that have adapted to localized environmental conditions.) You can plant a perennial meadow with wildflowers alone, but I expect that you will soon realize that something is missing; meadow wildflowers just don't look natural without native grasses. If you are tempted to include certain garden flowers or herbs in your meadow because you like them, be careful; some set prodigious crops of seeds or bulbs and can take over. I'm still hoeing out volunteers of anise hyssop, *Agastache foeniculum*, which I planted for the bees.

Perennial meadows can be whatever you wish them to be. For example, you might limit your choices to short-plant species — not a bad idea for small areas or meadows in housing developments where your neighborhood association scolds you if you skip a week in mowing your lawn. But if you use only short-stemmed plants, you miss out on the many wonderful long-stemmed wildflowers that can be cut for fresh and dried arrangements. Much of the charm of perennial meadows is in the season-long sequence of early, midseason, and late bloom. Your perennial meadow won't grow into a fully natural look for two or three years, until after the groups of plants have spread and filled in the bare

spots, and after wind, birds, and small animals have mixed up the picture by carrying seeds all around.

Siting the Meadow

MEADOWS need about the same full-sun situation as beds of annual and perennial garden flowers. In the South or warm West, afternoon shade helps, but it isn't absolutely necessary. Meadow flowers need good drainage to avoid root rot and

air movement to minimize foliage diseases, but they are not nearly as particular as garden flowers. As for organic matter, it isn't usually added, except to hard clay or sandy soils, which dry out so quickly that plants can't reach their full size or potential for color.

Even though their shade may not fall on the meadow, large trees nearby can send out roots to rob the flowers of water and plant nutrients. The rule of thumb is that tree roots extend to fill a circle about twice the size of that covered by the foliage canopy. So don't try to plant a meadow too close to a greedy tree, especially one that has a network of roots on or near the surface.

Where you situate your meadow depends in part on how much open land you have. Home-grown meadows come in all

Depending on the soil, certain meadow flowers will prevail over others. On fast-draining soil in Pennsylvania, perennial blanketflower and reseeding calliopsis, or prairie coreopsis, dominate the summer meadow.

sizes — as small as a flower bed tucked under a kitchen window or as large as the eye can encompass. The larger they are, the more effectively they convey the charm of a natural meadow. In a small to medium-size yard, the ideal place for a meadow is just beyond a patch of lawn, where it can show off against the smooth green turf. If you have the same love-hate relationship with your lawn as most Americans, you will welcome the opportunity to reduce its size to make room for a meadow.

On a larger property, place the meadow, if you can, where it can be glimpsed through trees or shrubs. Such locations are tantalizing; by revealing little and promising much, they draw more attention than immediate and full disclosure. Side yards are also effective sites. If trees or shrubs are spotted here and there, plant the open areas between them, but not where the flowers would be shaded all day or invaded by tree roots. Leave a narrow hidden path through the flowers, and hide a lawn chair under a shade tree surrounded by the meadow. When the flowers have grown to full height, you can sit in your little sanctuary and watch nature's other creatures play, feed, defend territories, or perish, if they are low on the food chain. You can savor the fragrance of the

A change of scenery: the same meadow just before fall frost, with goldenrods, New England aster, and a white aster, possibly *Aster pilosus* (frost aster), taking over.

flowers and imagine that you are the original man or woman in the original garden. You aren't, and it isn't, but your creation will be close enough to restore your faith in the natural order of things.

Most home gardens are flat, with little or no change in elevation. One dump-truck load of sandy soil can change the situation, if you have the energy to wheelbarrow it to your meadow site and build a broad, gently sloping, curving berm like an island. Make it twelve to eighteen inches high at the peak, and it will display your meadow as dramatically as a raised stage. The berm of sandy soil will warm up quickly and drain rapidly — just what most annuals and perennials like. (But you may have to do some hoeing or mulching the first year; the hauled-in soil might be full of weed seeds.) If you can't bring in soil conveniently, you can get what you need by what contractors call cutting and filling. Excavate an irregularly shaped basin to a depth of twelve to eighteen inches, pile the excavated soil behind it, line the depression with a plastic sheet, fill it with water, and plant marsh or water's-edge species in and around it. They will blend into the meadow surrounding them.

From a landscaping standpoint, an annual meadow looks more natural if it is backed up by a tree or shrub border than if it stands alone like an island in your lawn, but avoid planting too close to the root zones of trees. There is much to say for converting all the sunny areas in your back yard into a meadow, but do it gradually. It can be mind-blowing at first to look out your rear windows right into a sea of flowers — no lawn, no shrubs, just paths meandering through your meadow. And consider the visual effect when winter comes: not bad if you include native grasses in your meadow, but pretty dreary otherwise.

If you are eyeing your front yard as a site for a meadow, check with your local government to see if there are ordinances governing front-yard plantings; some municipalities do not take kindly to flowery meadows in front of homes. Meadows, perennial or annual, do grow tall, and after a windstorm or two can look informal or even messy, depending on your point of view. Their rugged insouciance and untamed appearance represent a threat to sensitive neighbors who panic at the sight of an innocent garter snake. You might want to start out with a small front-yard meadow and gradually expand it so that your neighbors become your allies rather than your opponents.

Wherever you place your meadow, it should be visible from an often-used window or patio, even if you can see just a corner of it. Your senses will respond not only to the bright and changing colors of the flowers but to their movement in the wind and to the butterflies and birds drawn to the food source.

If you position your meadow away from the house, you can delineate it from the lawn area with a picket or rail fence or old logs, which dovetail the two textures and enhance the "country" effect. Meander a trail through the meadow, not straight down your line of sight but curved so that it promises revelations of more color around the bend.

Siting a meadow for maximum effectiveness is easiest in country homes and grows progressively more difficult as you approach the crowded center of cities. It is difficult to imagine a more ideal situation for a meadow than along both sides of a lane leading to a country home. You can almost believe that you are in a Conestoga wagon cutting across clearings growing up in flowers. A tiny city meadow can be charming, but it strains credibility to believe that it just grew that way. Such a meadow is more symbolic than authentic. Still, a small meadow that fits into a corner formed by a wing of a house or thrives in the light shade of saplings on their way to becoming shade trees can give you a lot of satisfaction

Preparing the Soil for a Meadow

IF YOU have an underused vegetable or flower patch that has been cultivated for

White false indigo is a rugged competitor in roadside meadows. It shoots up slender spears through the grass and brush; once above them, it branches out and forms tall, often wavy spikes of pure white.

years, you can convert it to a meadow with few weed problems. However, if you work up a piece of lawn or idle land haphazardly and try to grow meadow flowers in it, you will get more weeds and grasses than flowers. Many a garden club and civic group has wasted its money trying to establish patches of meadow flowers in parks and along roadsides without adequately preparing the soil or monitoring the mowing. (Mowing at a height of four to five inches in early summer can discourage weeds and brush, but subsequent mowings should be delayed until after the seeds of annual flowers have dried and begun to shatter.)

Prepare soil for meadows in rather small increments. If you have sloping land, don't clear more than 5000 square feet a year, as heavy rains can cut gullies in large areas of exposed soil. Work the ground in the spring and remove debris and roots of perennial grasses. Forget about planting the same season. Instead, as weed and grass seedlings sprout, cultivate to a shallow depth to kill them. Continue with periodic shallow cultivations throughout the summer. Taking the time to cultivate frequently can greatly reduce problems with weeds and aggressive grasses, and eliminating weeds before you plant is much easier than coping with a heavy weed or grass crop soon after you sow seeds or transplant your perennials.

Between cultivations, take soil samples for testing by the Cooperative Extension Service. When you submit the samples, include a note saying that you intend to plant a meadow and do not need fertile soil. If your soil is quite acid — below pH 6.0 — the CES will probably recommend an application of dolomitic limestone to supply calcium and magnesium while raising the pH. If it recommends a fertilizer containing equal parts of nitrogen, phosphate, and potash (10-10-10, for example), ignore the recommendation and buy 0-10-10, or 5-10-10 at the most. Nitrogen, which is represented by the first number on the fertilizer analysis label, stimulates the germination of weed seeds. If your meadow area has been scalped of topsoil, don't use a chemical fertilizer, but mix in an organic fertilizer such as cottonseed or soybean meal at the rate of five pounds per hundred square feet to restore your soil without overstimulating weed growth.

When you convert a lawn area or an old garden space to a meadow, it usually isn't worth the expense of working in peat moss or pulverized pine bark. There are exceptions. If you have beastly hard clay or deep sand, adding a moderate amount of organic amendments can improve the germination, survival, and performance of wildflowers. The organic matter will aerate your soil and improve water penetration and retention while providing a better environment for helpful soil organisms, from bacteria and fungi to earthworms. On clay soil, work in an inch of organic matter and a couple of inches of sand. On sandy soil, incorporate an inch or two of organic matter. If you have a tiller, set it to dig as deep as possible and mix in the additives; if you use a spade, mix in the additives to spade depth.

GETTING RID OF WEEDS

THE MOST important consideration in preparing soils for meadows is minimizing weeds. There are ways to do it without using chemicals. In a lawn area, it is easiest to strip off the sod, where virtually all weed seeds are concentrated. This is practical and really not difficult when you have a typical cool-climate turf, such as bluegrass or red fescue. Simply cut the sod

into strips with a flat shovel, undercut it by shoving the shovel underneath, remove the strips, and pile them upside down to decompose into compost. With care, you can remove a layer only one to one and a half inches deep, which will leave most of the topsoil in place but dispose of most of the weed seeds.

However, you can't get rid of deep-rooted grasses and weeds such as Bermuda grass, quack grass, nutgrass, bindweed,

Perhaps America's favorite meadow flower, purple prairie coneflower, stays in bloom for weeks. Butterflies flock to it for nectar, and finches relish the dried seeds from its bristly seed heads.

The first flowers to bloom in this meadow near the sea are garden annuals such as toadflax, baby's-breath, and Shirley poppies.

recommend it for seeds of most perennial wildflowers. These germinate slowly, sometimes over a period of several weeks, and the seedlings remain small for some time. In all but the coldest areas of the country, one of the best ways to start perennial wildflowers and native grasses from seeds is in an outdoor nursery, which protects seeds from excessive drying from wind or intense sunlight, washing away, birds, insects, slugs, snails, pets, and foot traffic. You can convert a picnic table into

Showy evening primrose is a low-growing, spreading flower of meadows and prairies. Durable and drought-resistant, it bears white blossoms in early spring, which gradually turn pink.

a nursery, or make a table from cinder blocks and exterior plywood or, even better, hardware cloth stapled over a pressure-treated lumber frame. Use special near-sterile seed-starting soil for filling pots or flats and you will experience fewer

Robert Lyons developed this fast, weed-free way to grow a flowery meadow:

Start pinches of a meadow seed mixture in pots; cover lightly with vermiculite or milled sphagnum moss.

Within three weeks the pots will be filled with a dense stand of flower seedlings.

Regular feeding and watering will bring the seedlings along rapidly.

Transplant clumps of seedlings into prepared and leveled soil. Space clumps eighteen inches apart. Cover the bare soil with two inches of pine or hardwood bark mulch.

Three weeks later, the thick stand of seedlings within each clump will force early bloom.

Six weeks after planting, the mulch is no longer visible; the flowers have filled in solidly. Calliopsis, baby's-breath, and baby-blue-eyes are in bloom.

CHAPTER 4

Prairies

Rattlesnake-master and prairie coneflower look as good as a grouping of cultivated perennials. Guy Sternberg, a landscape architect, planted this bed of prairie flowers in Springfield, Illinois.

NO LANDSCAPE so evokes the American past as the prairie — those endless open spaces and rolling plains covered with waving grasses, buffalo pastures that separate the midwestern woods from the Rocky Mountains. Settlers leaving Kansas City by prairie schooner during the spring set sail on a sea of early-blooming flowers: violets, phlox, buttercups, prairie dandelions, windflowers, and the curious *Geum triflorum*, called prairie smoke. By midsummer the grass would be waist high, but not high enough to hide the various milkweeds, the leguminous sennas and wild indigos, the golden waves, coneflowers, blazing stars, and black-eyed Susans, and the bizarre *Eryngium* called rattlesnake-master. With the appearance of the tall, late-blooming silphiums, with their intricately adapted foliage, and the many species of sunflowers, asters, and goldenrods, the wagon master would increase the pace to reach the forts at the foot of the Rockies before heavy snowfall.

Natural prairies such as these are almost as rare today as a real prairie schooner; only small relicts survive to serve as models for the growing movement in prairie restoration. Although no one pretends that we can re-create the historic prairie, we can hope to bring its sense of place into our lives and those of our children. Even when nostalgia for the past is not a motivating factor, city dwellers and suburbanites in the upper and central Midwest are moved to plant home-garden "prairies" or prairie flowers among their perennials. They see the prairie landscape style as a sensible, attractive alternative to monotonous, sterile lawns and "low maintenance" foundation shrubs, and to the fertilizers, chemicals, and fossil fuels required to maintain them. Such gardeners are disappointed that their conventional landscapes attract few birds and butterflies, and they want to change their environment to halt the decline in the population of wildlife.

In 1989 I was among a group of garden writers who traveled to the University of Wisconsin Arboretum at Madison, where the staff divided us into small groups and led us into a sixty-five-acre prairie constructed from scratch. It was late summer, and dozens of flowering species native to Wisconsin prairies were in bloom, some towering well above our heads. In the tallgrass prairie, herbaceous wildflowers filled in between clumps of big bluestem and Indian grass. The sights, sounds, and mood of the place made a lasting impression on all of us, as did the devoted scientists who brought an abandoned horse pasture back to what settlers might have seen from their wagons.

These ecologists explained that special kinds of flowers evolved to coexist with the cover of native prairie grasses. The smaller wildflowers grow and mature quickly, producing their seeds or replenishing food reserves in rootstocks before being overwhelmed by larger grasses and flowers. Just as their color fades, the taller wildflowers begin to blossom, reaching above the thick basal growth of the grasses to attract pollinating insects. Successive waves of flower species follow, each taller than its predecessor, stretching to stay ahead of the grasses. For their part, the native grasses serve as sturdy big

---

At the University of Wisconsin Arboretum at Madison, tall prairie grasses help to support the soon-to-be head-high prairie dock and compass plant. The early-blooming *Phlox* species and rattlesnake-master will be overgrown but will endure.

ar
th

w
te
in
m
th
on
al

The next year he could hardly believe his eyes: more than a dozen species of wildflowers bloomed there. Elderly residents vowed that they hadn't seen those flowers along that road in more than thirty years!

How to go about restoring a prairie depends on its size. For larger areas, the practical approach is to retain one of the nurseries, environmental designers, or consulting ecologists who specialize in prairie plantings. Most homeowners dealing with areas of one acre or less can do the job with typical garden power equipment and hand tools. However, most people prefer to create a prairie rather than attempt a restoration. If you start from scratch, you can plant your prairie with native species to suit your individual taste rather than with a mixture of species that might have grown on the property before the settlers came.

❧ STARTING FROM SEEDS

IF YOU are already using fluorescent lights for starting seedlings of vegetable, flower, and herb plants, you can also use them for germinating seeds of prairie species and growing the plants to transplanting stage. However, you can get equally

Seed companies are evaluating prairie flowers for garden potential. This annual flower, growing in Maine and labeled "prairie aster," may be the prairie native *Machaeranthera tanacetifolia* (tahoka daisy), a close relative of the asters.

good results by starting your wildflower and grass seeds in pots outdoors from spring through summer; you don't need a greenhouse. Fill four-inch pots with moistened potting soil and pack them close together in carrying trays. Plant three to six seeds per pot, cover them to a depth equal to three times the diameter of the seeds, and firm the soil gently to establish a moisture bond between the seeds and the soil. Set the trays on a table outdoors where they won't be damaged, and cover the seedlings with a floating row cover to protect them from insects and birds. Water daily with a fine spray; water will go right through the porous spunbonded fabric.

Start seeds in the spring in northern climates, in late summer where winters are relatively mild. As soon as one crop has grown large enough for transplanting, start another. The price of an ounce of seeds each of several species for starting in pots is minuscule compared to that of the pounds of seeds you need for direct seeding, and transplanting gives you better control of the mixture of species. Direct seeding tends to favor the species that sprout quickly and grow rapidly.

BUYING SEEDS OR PLANTS

TO SELECT seeds or plants of prairie wildflowers and grasses, send for catalogues from specialists in prairie species — not generalists who throw the prairie species in with garden flowers and canned seed mixtures, but companies that deal exclusively in prairie grasses and wildflowers. They sell seeds of prairie, woodland-edge, and wetland species separately by species or blend them into mixtures.

PREPARING THE SOIL

PREPARING the soil for prairie plantings is quite different from getting it ready for vegetables and flowers. The majority of prairie flowers prefer a rather dry, nutrient-poor soil. Prime farmland, rich and moisture-retentive, tends to foster weeds.

If you intend to start your prairie by putting in plants, the easiest and best way to prepare the soil is to let the land grow up in weeds and grasses, freeze down during the winter, and dry off in the spring. Then, after notifying your neighbors and the fire department, burn it. Hook up water hoses and have them running before you set fire to the grass. Burning is especially recommended if your ground is infested with thistles. However, if the prairie site abuts your house, or if your neighbors object to burning, mow the vegetation to the ground in the spring and let the litter lie, to serve as a mulch.

Purchase or propagate plants of low-growing species if your area is small, or a mixture of tall and short species if your plot is sizable. If your soil is fairly well drained, dig planting holes, set the transplants in place, and back-fill with the native soil. If your soil is heavy, compacted clay, mix equal parts of peat moss or ground pine bark and clean sand into it. Dig planting holes the size of a bucket, set the plants slightly higher than the surrounding soil, and fill around them with the mixture, firming it around the root balls. Keep a hose handy to water the seedlings every day or two until they show signs of new growth. If you have the time, water each individual plant rather than turning the sprinkler on the area. Sprinkling will bring up weeds that you will have to hoe out.

Preparing the soil for direct seeding is almost as easy. Start by tilling in the spring, as soon as the ground is dry enough to work. Set your tiller deep enough to uproot any deep-rooted weeds and fleshy-rooted grasses. Remove weeds and trash, roughly level the soil, and let it lie until a rain or sprinkling brings up a crop of weed and grass seedlings. Go over the area with a push-pull or action hoe to cut these weed seedlings off just below the surface of the soil. Don't cultivate deeply or you will bring a new crop of weed seeds to the surface, where they will germinate. Let a second crop of weed and grass seeds germinate and repeat the shallow cultivation. Your ground is now ready for planting, but don't fertilize it: the nitrogen in fertilizer would stimulate the growth of weeds.

As an alternative to working up the entire area for direct seeding, you can dig patches two or three feet across with a spade. Space the patches irregularly, six to twelve feet apart. If the soil is heavy clay, mix a two-inch layer of peat moss or ground pine bark and sand into the patches to raise the level for better drainage. Direct-seed or transplant seedlings of individual species in the patches to establish drifts of color and mounds of grasses. After you broadcast seeds over the rough soil in cleared areas, walk on it to firm them into contact with the soil, and cover with a thin mulch of straw. Don't attempt to bring up the seeds by watering; let rain germinate them. When the seedlings grow enough for you to distinguish the perimeters of the patches, cultivate around them with a push-pull hoe to kill weeds.

As the islands of prairie species begin to expand, help them take over by gradually cleaning off the soil between the established patches. Leave it rough so the seeds of the prairie species can lodge on the seedbed and take hold. Grub out any woody plants that emerge and ruthlessly prune the roots of pushy species such as goldenrod. You may find it handy to make "sneak paths," narrow, curving aisles like game trails, across the line of sight so they are almost invisible. Via sneak paths, you can reach the various corners of your planting without stepping on prairie flowers or compacting the soil around them. You can plant the paths with seeds of buffalo grass, a low-growing, sod-forming species from the shortgrass prairie, or cover them with gravel over porous synthetic landscape cloth. If you intend to burn your prairie, make the gravel layer deep enough to protect the plastic weed barrier from fire damage.

All-year interest at the demonstration prairie at the Chicago Botanic Garden. In early spring the many perennial flowers and grasses show several shades of green. The earliest flowers are just beginning to open.

Native grasses are very much a part
of the botanic garden's prairie. Notice
how they complement the asters and
goldenrods in the fall. The dried seed
heads will attract birds.

In winter, the plants provide cover and food for birds and small animals.

Maintaining a Prairie

IT WAS long believed that the ash produced by fires on prairies was essential to their maintenance. However, research has shown that mowing the winter-dormant growth and raking it off to expose the soil is also effective in stimulating growth — welcome news to homeowners who want to grow prairies close to their houses. Mow the prairie in early winter, after the birds have eaten their fill of seeds, and leave the mulch in place to protect the crowns of seedlings. Set your mower as high as it can be adjusted. Use a push mower; the weight of a riding mower can compact the soil. If the stems of grasses and flowers are too thick and heavy for your mower to manage, hand-cut your prairie with a scythe, a sickle, or a serrated swing-blade weeder. Commercial landscapers have begun to use gasoline-powered weed whackers equipped with jointed metal flails in place of monofilament line, which frays or breaks when used on heavy weed and grass stems.

Remove and compost the mulch in early spring to let the soil warm up. This will add a few weeks to the growing season at a time when soil moisture conditions are good for growth. The early warming activates the soil bacteria that decompose organic matter and liberate plant nutrients. Roots are the major contribution of prairie plants to the soil; their massive systems gradually die in place and are replaced. Prairie ants and earthworms also make an important contribution to soil by bringing nutrient-laden particles of subsoil to the surface.

If your prairie is growing on poor soil, a light spring application of organic fertilizer will help stimulate growth. Pull out large, coarse weeds before they set seeds, and dig out the sprouts of woody plants. If certain vigorous species threaten to spread widely, prune their roots with a spade and pull out and remove the runners. Other than doing that, and plugging in new species as you grow the plants, you should be able to let the prairie take care of itself. It won't need watering except during periods of extended drought, and then only to keep it in flower.

Talk Up Prairies

IF YOU work for a midwestern company with a large landscaped area and are in a position to influence policies, suggest that your firm convert some of its turf area to prairie. Have the prairie installed by a specialist and watch the positive impact the flowers, grasses, birds, and butterflies have on employee morale.

Missouri primrose has much to commend it. Low-growing, it has attractive foliage, very large flowers, decorative seedpods, and a rugged constitution. It is very adaptable.

CHAPTER 5

Western Wildflower Gardens

White prickly poppy grows in large colonies on disturbed land or on dry sandy or gravelly pastures that have been overgrazed. It can be an annual or a biennial; sow seeds in the fall.

WEST OF the shortgrass prairie lies some of the best country for growing wildflowers, and some of the toughest. Except for the Pacific Northwest west of the Cascades and a narrow coastal strip in northern California, the West receives less than half the rainfall enjoyed by the rest of the country. In high-altitude areas, much of the annual precipitation comes in the form of snow. In arid parts of the West, the scanty rainfall is not sufficient to leach away the salts that accumulate from evaporating water, and the soil becomes alkaline.

Often the water supply has a high content of mineral salts, which aggravates the problem.

It may help you visualize western wildflower opportunities if you view the West as having four very different climates. I know there are many more, for I lived and gardened in California for many years and monitored seed crops in several western states. Yet four climates should suffice to illustrate why western species grow well within their native ranges but don't always thrive in other parts of North America, and why gardeners in the West would be well advised to grow their native plants rather than continue to try to emulate the landscapes of England or the eastern United States.

The Mediterranean Climate of California

IN ITS lowlands and foothills, California has distinct wet and dry seasons and elevated winter temperatures, much like the climate of Mediterranean countries. Yet because of locally sparse winter rainfall and low summer humidity, much of California is desert country. It isn't like the desert of the movies, with Sahara sand, one-humped camels, and an occasional oasis, but you can't grow agricultural row crops or maintain conventional landscapes without irrigation. Before overgrazing upset the ecology, much of the state was carpeted with seasonally green grass and wildflowers. Now brush covers many of the rolling hills and lower mountains.

It would seem logical for Californians to adapt to their climate and plant native trees, shrubs, ground covers, and wildflowers that can get by with little or no supplemental irrigation. Most haven't. Whenever periodic back-to-back droughts shrink reservoirs, nurseries that specialize in native plants enjoy a boom in business. But as soon as a wet winter brings water supplies back to normal, people revert to buying water-wasteful exotic plants and lavishing water on manicured lawns. You can drive down the streets of any California suburb and see more species of trees, shrubs, and ground covers native to South Africa, Australia, New Zealand, and Asia than grow wild in the Golden State.

California has several excellent botanical gardens where native shrubs, trees, and wildflowers are displayed in landscaping situations. One of the best places to learn about wildflowers from all over the state is the Menzies Wildflower Garden in San Francisco's Strybing Arboretum, designed by landscape architect Ron Lutsko, Jr. California is also home to such excellent magazines as *Sunset* and *Pacific Horticulture*, which have long advocated environmental landscaping. Yet ironically, the landscaping that has come to be known as "California style" depends more on structures, stones, pools, and accessories than on California's native plants. This is really quite sad, for by using only native plants, the state's home and commercial landscapers could create designs that would use little water, require minimum maintenance, and have a look that is uniquely "California."

If you live in one of the other forty-nine states and have wondered why Californian wildflowers grow only so-so for you, the reason is that you can't match California habitats. No other place in the United States offers such a combination of mild winter temperatures, concentrated winter rainfall, and long, dry summers. Perennial and biennial species native to California may grow poorly in humid climates because they have adapted to seasonally dry soils; they can die where summer rains saturate the ground.

Here's how the climate in California determines the growth of wildflowers. Most of the rain comes from November through April, and virtually none in other months. Slopes facing west get the most rain when moist air from the Pacific is forced up into cooler strata and condenses. Southern California is much more dependent on storms blowing northeast from the Mexican coast; there, rains are infrequent, often heavy, and may come in late summer and fall rather than throughout the winter, as in northern California.

Winter rains and the shielding effect of high mountains to the north and east elevate average winter temperatures. Over eons of time, wildflowers developed special survival strategies as they evolved within this unusual climate. Some grow as winter annuals; their seeds germinate during the fall rains, grow slowly through the winter, flourish with the coming of longer, warmer spring days, and blossom just before nature turns off the water faucet. Certain species of annual wildflowers can be found at low elevations and in the foothills over the entire state. Others are more restricted in distribution, and a few are found in narrow ecological niches.

The biennial and perennial wildflowers that grow among the annuals at lower elevations have evolved different survival strategies. They send down deep roots to draw water from lower soil strata. Some have gray or silvery leaves coated with down, very narrow leaves, succulent foliage, or leaves with a high content of resin, all of which are devices to reduce evaporation. These are difficult to grow except in other Mediterranean climates, as any easterner who has tried to grow the perennial matilija poppy or fried-egg plant, *Romneya coulteri*, can testify. California biennials are opportunistic; if conditions are near-perfect, they may act like short-lived perennials. Several California wildflower species form bulbs, tubers, or other fleshy underground parts to carry them through the long dry season, when their tops usually dry, shrivel, and disappear.

The many microclimates of California have produced more species of plants than any other state, and especially wildflowers, including woody subshrubs. Some species, such as the California poppy,

Eschscholzia californica, flower spottily during the winter, but the major show of color doesn't come until March or April, especially from the annuals. The length of the flowering season is largely dependent on the amount and duration of winter rain. The great fields of annuals — California poppies; lupines; tidy-tips, *Layia platyglossa*; goldfields, *Lasthenia californica* (= *L. chrysostoma*); blazing stars, *Mentzelia laevicaulis*; clarkias; and a great many others — flower in the spring and set seeds and dry up in late May or June. Each spring the residents of California's cities make pilgrimages to the hills around inland valleys to view them. The dry summers help maintain the vitality of the seeds, which renew the natural fields of wildflowers every year.

In areas where as little as ten or twelve inches of rain may fall during the winter, you see many species of drought-resistant tender perennials, some with gray or silver leaves, growing among the drought-tolerant annuals, such as the *Argemone* species called prickly poppies. Especially beautiful and attractive to hummingbirds are the many tender perennial penstemons and the aptly named hummingbird flower, *Epilobium canum* subspp. *angustifolium* (= *Zauschneria californica*). The shrubby California buckwheat, *Eriogonum fasciculatum*, and golden yarrow, *Eriophyllum confertiflorum*, can be seen along country roadsides.

Up on the coastal ranges and in the foothills to the timbered elevations of the

sierras, where rain or snowfall is heavier, you find wild irises, lilies, and shrubby plants: California lilac, *Ceanothus* spp.; manzanita, *Arctostaphylos* spp.; and the ubiquitous mixed brush called chaparral, which can endure the long summer months with little or no rainfall. Shade-tolerant flowers are relatively few but

beautiful, including coral-bells, *Heuchera sanguinea*; western shooting-star, *Dodecatheon clevelandii*; and a few distinct California species of forest-floor wildflowers well known in the East, such as trillium and wild ginger. I can recall my astonishment at stumbling upon a large colony of giant trilliums in a moist,

California's dry summers turn the native bunchgrasses an attractive straw brown while the last of the winter annual wildflowers bloom among them.

wooded ravine near Cupertino, California. Until that time I had considered trilliums exclusively an eastern woodland flower.

For all practical purposes, the alpine plants that grow above the timberline in California's mountains are better left to hobbyists who can meet their exacting requirements for perfect drainage, cool temperatures, and moderate humidity. Other California species that are difficult to grow elsewhere include the many wildflowers that are indigenous to the serpentine rock that laces California's mountains and foothills. They have adapted to a rather skewed ratio of plant nutrients that would be difficult to duplicate.

The water supply in California is finite. As I am writing this, California's farmers are having their allotments for irrigation water reduced by as much as 70 percent because of a long-term drought. There could be no more convincing argument for reducing the large expanses of turf that account for much of the residential water use in the state. It will make a profound difference in the appearance of Californian landscapes when the turf is replaced in large part by clumps of perennial native wildflowers, ornamental native grasses, and native shrubs and ground covers, interspersed with colorful winter annuals. One can only trust that when the state's inhabitants begin replacing lawns with wildflowers, they will have the foresight to avoid planting exotic ornamental grasses and herbaceous plants, which are already escaping to threaten their wild land. (The Santa Monica Mountains chapter of the California Native Plant Society has compiled a list of these "thugs"; you

can get it by writing to the address for the society in Appendix III.)

Any California gardener who wishes to plant native wildflowers should start by improving his or her soil with organic matter, which allows water to penetrate soil faster, improves water retention and drainage, and enlivens soil organisms. It should be well decomposed, as lignin breaks down slowly in dry soil. In addition to being universally deficient in organic matter, California soils are usually short on available nitrogen. When preparing ground for fall planting of wildflower seeds, gardeners should incorporate a light application of an organic fertilizer, so the plants develop a large enough frame to support an abundance of flowers. When I gardened in California, one of the most desirable soil conditioners was rice hulls composted with chicken manure. If you use it, no supplemental nitrogen should be necessary. (A few wildflower species that grow in California's yellow pine forests require an eight- to ten-inch layer of grit for good growth. Organic matter and fertilizer should not be added.)

California wildflowers are well known across North America by gardeners who have never visited the West. They make up the majority of the native North American species included in packages of many meadow seed mixtures. Despite my ambivalent feelings about planting wildflowers outside their native areas, I can't see that planting eastern meadows with California wildflowers will harm the environment in any way, since these flowers won't repeat in most climates (except in dry parts of the Southwest) and don't tend to become agricultural pests or displace native flowers. The brilliance of California wildflowers and their wide range of clear colors is unsurpassed; temporary meadows of great beauty can be created with them. However, I recommend planting patches of separate species, rather than a mixture of seeds of several species, to get an authentic meadow effect. Outside California, you will have the best success with these native wildflowers if you live in an area with cool summers, in the Southwest, or along the Gulf Coast on sandy soil, where fall planting will bring winter or early spring color. The poorest results will come from spring planting where summers are warm and wet; in this case, California wildflowers will die after a brief show of color. (See Chapter 8 for a list of California wildflowers that are relatively easy to grow elsewhere, prepared by George Waters, editor of *Pacific Horticulture*.)

The native California species of iris grow during the winter rainy season, bloom in the spring, and go dormant in the dry summer months.

The Desert Southwest

THE OLD saw about any generalization being dangerous certainly applies when one lumps the entire Southwest into a single category. The climates and soil types from the Mojave Desert to west Texas are even more diverse than those of coastal and northern California. The only universal feature is dryness — dry soil and dry air. You cannot conceive of the speed at which dry desert air can suck moisture out of the soil until you compare flowers growing in the lee of a wall or fence with similar flowers exposed to drying winds.

Prevailing temperatures depend largely on the elevation of the garden. Although people tend to gravitate to the low desert for winter warmth, far more land area lies at upper elevations, where it is too cold for the signature plants of the warm desert, saguaro cacti and Joshua trees. Easterners who tend to judge the Southwest from winter visits to Phoenix would be surprised at the extremely cold winters of the high desert, and they would leave the low desert posthaste if subjected to a few hours of its summer heat without air conditioning. Other parts of the United States have greater differences between maximum and minimum temperatures, but they also have the tempering effect of higher humidity and winter snow cover.

This land of extremes shelters an unbelievable array of specialized wildflowers in niches created by differences in elevation and terrain, rainfall or the lack of it, shelter from the wind, drainage, and soil pH. Plant families that are abundant in the deserts of northern Mexico cross the border with impunity to multiply in similar environments. Plant families that are thinly represented among the eastern wildflowers — the four o'clock family, or *Nyctaginaceae*, for example — have evolved several southwestern species.

Rainfall in the dry Southwest is very sparse, and often comes in late summer and fall cloudbursts. When it does, a spectacular show of color follows, but in the high desert it is occasionally cut short by cold weather. Winters in low desert country are short and rather mild but cold enough at times to freeze back tender plants; the lower the elevation, the less dieback due to frost. The basic desert wildflowers are the very deep-rooted bushy or shrubby perennials, cacti and other succulents, and many species of precocious annuals that are capable of flowering and setting seeds rapidly after a rain. Some of these species are quite site-specific and don't travel well. They are accustomed to very dry, usually alkaline, sometimes gravelly or rocky soil. There are exceptions; along the few creeks and rivers you can find swamp species quite similar to eastern wildflowers that like wet feet.

Standing cypress prefers dry sandy or gravelly soil containing lime. A biennial, it sows seeds in the fall.

Desert mariposa requires perfect drainage and winter mulching where temperatures fluctuate widely.

For many years southwestern nurserymen generally ignored the landscape potential of native species. They found it easier to please new gardeners from the East by selling them familiar eastern species and by following eastern landscape styles, which were originally developed in Europe. Occasionally they would inject a token cactus or a yucca into the greenery or make a corner of the landscape into a "native plant garden," which hardly improved matters. It took the working examples provided at the desert botanical gardens and a new breed of environmentally sensitive nurserymen to begin to change southwestern landscape designs and plant choices. Judith and Roland Phillips are good examples.

The Phillipses grew up in the East and Midwest. When they moved to New Mexico, south of Albuquerque, they were shocked by the lack of concern about environmental landscaping. Judith began

In southern New Mexico, drought-resistant native shrubs anchor the sand and enable wildflowers such as white-tufted evening primrose and various species of penstemon to take hold.

designing appropriate, water-conserving landscapes, but couldn't find enough native New Mexican plants at nurseries. She and Roland had to pioneer in locating seed sources, evaluating species for adaptability beyond their local habitats, and propagating them commercially. After years of missionary work, Judith has convinced many settlers from the East not to attempt to duplicate the inappropriate, water-wasteful styles of gardens and lawns they had back home. At the Phillipses' Veguita, New Mexico, nursery, where the drying winds are almost ceaseless, Judith uses shrubby windbreaks to create shelterbelts where wildflowers can thrive, and she groups native shrubs to anchor the sand. Around these islands she plants native southwestern wildflowers.

Judith advises gardeners in the Southwest to devote a lot of thought to moderating the impact of the intense sun, drying winds, and alkaline soil and water. She doesn't use ramadas, the slatted shade structures seen in the low desert, but prefers to use the shade and shelter of native trees, large shrubs, walls, stones, and hillsides. She applies organic mulches to reduce evaporation, but contrary to eastern soil improvement practices, she seldom incorporates organic matter into the soil, except when planting lawns of native grasses. It has been her experience that

Texas bluebonnet and Drummond phlox bloom with evening primrose along a rangeland fence.

doing so results in lush growth of perennial species that are accustomed to growing slowly in rather poor, gritty soil. When they are pushed with organic matter, they don't live long. Without it, they become hard, durable plants that will thrive for years.

Like other southwestern gardeners, Judith has learned not to use sprinkler irrigation, which is inefficient and can leave unsightly salt encrustations and stains on fences, stones, and walks. Drip irrigation is efficient, but where the water is extremely salty, gardeners may have to flood their gardens periodically to dissolve sur-

A tender yellow-flowered perennial native to Texas and the Southwest, desert marigold gets another of its common names, paper-daisy, from its petals, which turn translucent when dry.

face salts and leach them down to lower layers of the soil. From my experience in western seed fields, I can vouch that there isn't much else you can do to modify the pH of alkaline soils. Regardless of treatments, neutral or alkaline soils tend to remain that way. Sulfur and aluminum sulfate can temporarily drop the pH of the cultivated layer, but it will rise as salts from lower layers are drawn up with water

Fragrant Texas bluebonnet is a winter annual and will grow well only in places with mild winters. It likes lime in the soil and grows best if the seeds are inoculated.

responding to capillary pull. As the water evaporates, it will leave concentrations of sodium, calcium, and magnesium combined with chemical bases as salts. This problem can become extremely severe in dry desert areas and is often exacerbated by high salt concentrations in water supplies. Some gardeners have been driven to growing flowers in containers of artificial soil, which can be flushed periodically to lower the salt content. Fortunately, the winter rains over much of the West dissolve most of the salts accumulated during the summer and drive them down to lower layers in the soil.

Judith introduced me to several perennial southwestern wildflowers that are little known elsewhere. When these are grown in the East, they are often treated as annuals. None will repeat reliably where winters are long and summers are rainy, but some are more heat-resistant than California wildflowers and thus are somewhat more adaptable. Among these are blackfoot daisy, *Melampodium leucanthum*; desert marigold, *Baileya multiradiata* (also found in California); desert zinnia, *Zinnia grandiflora*; purple prairie clover, *Petalostemon purpureum* or *Dalea purpurea* (also found in the Plains states); and scarlet globe mallow, *Sphaeralcea coccinea*.

Some of the hardy perennial wildflowers from higher elevations in the Southwest will live over in the northern areas of the East, where they are protected by snow cover, but they must have perfect drainage. Actually, some botanical gardens in the East are just getting around to evaluating the hardiness and performance of desert perennials. It will be interesting to see how the one eastern species of hummingbird, the ruby-throat, will take to western wildflowers, which collectively attract fifteen hummingbird species! (See Chapter 8 for a list of southwestern wildflowers prepared by Judith Phillips.)

High-Altitude Western Wildflowers

AS YOU climb from the low, warm-climate areas of the West into the foothills, mountain benches, and upland valleys, the growing season becomes progressively shorter and cooler. The major population centers in the mountains are at altitudes of 4000 to 6000 feet, where, except for the need for irrigation and supplementary organic matter, gardening doesn't differ greatly from gardening in midwestern areas. Snowfall is light to moderate, and summer nights are cooler. Only a few cities of significant size are at higher altitudes, along with vacation homes, ski villages, and the year-round residences of hardy types who can cope with occasional spring snowstorms.

It is a tribute to the beauty of high-altitude western wildflowers that gardeners all over the world want to try growing them. Where summers are relatively cool, it isn't all that difficult, but you need to understand a bit about their habitats. As you travel from lowland western areas up toward the timberline, the dominant flowers shift from reseeding annuals to deep-rooted perennials, which are better suited

The Colorado state flower, *Aquilegia caerulea*, is one of the parents of many garden columbine hybrids.

to surviving the long, often snowy winters and the late summer droughts that can come after the snowmelt groundwater has been exhausted. In the jumble of soil types and microclimates on high mountain slopes, you see many kinds of perennial subalpine, alpine, and tundra wildflowers that have adapted to demanding habitats: taluses, screes, deep gravel, rock crevices, protected valleys, wind-blasted slopes, and streamsides. Generally, highland soils are low in organic matter and available nutrients.

Operating from food reserves stored in their heavy root systems, some of the perennials begin blooming early — the types that send up bloom stalks before forming sizable plants. Early bloom is essential to survival at very high altitudes, where the growing season may be only sixty to ninety days long. At moderately high elevations you see more legumes, deep-rooted woody subshrubs, and the many wildflower species that form large plants before blooming in summer or fall.

Visitors to the highland West especially enjoy the columbines, white-tufted evening primroses, and many penstemon and lupine species. At medium-high elevations, the fall season brings a great show of color from the perennial asters, gayfeathers, and goldenrods — much the same array as enjoyed in the East. Some of the perennials, such as lupines, penstemons, and columbines, will grow well elsewhere if summers are cool and perfect drainage is supplied. The annual wildflower species from lower mountain slopes will grow surprisingly well in the northern half of the United States and Canada but can't endure hot, humid summers. In their native habitat they volunteer each year from seeds dropped the previous season, but few will repeat in warmer, more humid climates.

Gardeners in the major mountain cities of the West have a good track record for using native plants, but when you drive down their streets, your first impression is of transplanted eastern garden styles. That's a fair assessment, because with the aid of summer irrigation, many exotic hardy perennials and shrubs grow well in the western mountains. (Denver winters, for example, are milder than those in the upper Midwest.) Also, until mountain cities began to boom in population, there was ample water for lawns and English-style mixed borders of shrubs and perennials. Typically, mountain gardeners used their native wildflowers as they did the cultivated annuals and perennials, to create mixed borders.

Now water is becoming acutely short in some mountainous areas, and expensive virtually everywhere. Unfortunately, the useful term "xeriscaping" is often misinterpreted as representing a sere, austere style of landscaping that incorporates species native to areas of extremely low rainfall. In high mountain areas there is no need for such a sacrificial approach. Although some gardeners water occasionally to maintain continuous color, the residual moisture from snowmelt is sufficient to support native annual and perennial wildflowers through their season of bloom; then a variety of drought-tolerant native shrubs and trees can take over. In and around major mountain cities, however, where growing seasons average four to five months in length and summers are rainless except for occasional thunderstorms, gardeners may have to irrigate as often as every two or three days, especially during dry, windy weather. Most gardeners aren't aware of the need to irrigate during the typically dry, snowless winters, but desiccation kills more plants in the high mountains (especially older woody plants) than low temperatures do. Relatively new plants are more vigorous, and their pliable tissue seems to resist splitting and drying. The worst-case scenario in mountain gardening comes when severe cold, zero degrees or below, arrives in November or December, when plants are not fully dormant; this can kill or damage many plants despite their inherent hardiness.

Lawns are a luxury — in a windy, dry mountain climate, a lawn will begin demanding at least weekly watering as soon as groundwater levels begin to drop in late spring and will keep on demanding it until the ground begins to freeze. Water use could be minimized if gardeners planted drought-tolerant native grasses, but most prefer the manicured look of bluegrass and fine-leaved fescue, despite the cost in water, herbicides, and fertilizers.

Some of the relatively low intermountain valleys, such as central Utah and the Snake River Valley of Idaho, have less snowfall and warmer, drier summers than higher elevations do. Their summers are fairly long and frost-free. By July their soils are so dry that the native grasses begin to turn brown. Only deep-rooted perennial plants can endure without irrigation. Gardeners there can become frustrated, because their climate is nearly perfect for growing a tremendous variety of flowers, native and exotic, yet except in agricultural communities that hold first rights to irrigation, water is so scarce and expensive that maintaining large flower and shrub borders and lawns is difficult.

High-altitude gardeners in the West have to cope not only with water shortages but with drying winds, late frosts, and extremely short, cool growing seasons. Their soil is often near neutral in reaction and is always low in organic matter. Rock-garden specialists, who are the most active group in growing western wildflowers from seeds, have learned that starting seeds in cold frames produces hardy seedlings that don't require hardening off. They sow seeds in January or February, and the bright winter sun generates enough heat to germinate the seeds within two to four weeks. The seedlings grow slowly but branch heavily and produce strong root systems, and they are ready for transplanting after eight to twelve weeks.

Mountain gardeners learn to adjust their plant lists and cultural practices to their local microclimates and soil. They grow native species that shrug off late spring frosts; they incorporate organic matter in their soil to increase its water-holding capacity; they use drip irrigation to save water; and they minimize evaporation by mulching and planting downwind from structures and shrub windbreaks.

Robert Heapes, a nationally known photographer of flowers and a botanical historian, has filled an extensive rock garden at Parker, Colorado, with more than six hundred species of plants from all over the world. His plant collection is especially rich in species native to the several western mountain ranges and to Mexico. Because Bob has to keep his garden in condition for photographs, he irrigates fairly often, plant by plant, to meet the needs not only of each species but of each individual plant. He has hauled in sand to make his soil drain faster, so he seldom loses plants to root rot. If you have tried to grow western wildflowers, only to see them die suddenly, the problem may lie with poor drainage in dense soil; the plants suffocate from lack of oxygen when it is displaced in the soil by water. You can get around the problem as Bob did, by adding sand or a combination of sand and organic matter. Raised beds are another option for improving drainage, but in the West they can make the soil dry out too quickly.

Bob's garden is picturesque, with huge rocks, steep grades, and narrow trails. It is

densely planted, to the extent that when Bob wants to add a new species, he has to take out a less desirable plant to make room. Yet it is environmentally sound and, with a small lawn of native bunch-grasses, requires relatively little water. If you were to seek the perfect high-altitude flower garden, you might not find a better one.

Bob recommends these relatively easy-to-grow native perennial species as starter plants in high-altitude gardens: bitterroot, *Lewisia cotyledon*; Rocky Mountain blue columbine, *Aquilegia caerulea*; golden banner, *Thermopsis divaricarpa*; and the widely adapted perennial vervain, *Verbena canadensis*. To attract humming-birds, he recommends the somewhat more difficult orange zauschneria, *Epilobium canum* subsp. *garrettii* (= *Zauschneria garrettii*), and Cascade penstemon, *Penstemon cardwellii*. Such annuals as clark-ia, *Clarkia pulchella*, and baby-blue-eyes, *Nemophila menziesii*, make good fillers to cover bare ground while the perennials are bushing out. (See Chapter 8 for Bob's longer list of recommended high-altitude wildflowers.)

I mentioned to Bob my clear memory of mules'-ears, *Wyethia amplexicaulis*, which I saw when driving over a pass from the south into Logan, Utah. It looks like a

This high-altitude garden in Colorado combines several adapted cultivars of exotic rock-garden plants with wild species grown from seeds collected all over the West and Mexico.

dwarf sunflower with shiny leaves. "Difficult, and too big for most gardens" was his response. I have the room for big plants, but if mules'-ears is difficult for him, it would be impossible for me!

Western gardeners are fortunate to have access to several mail-order nurseries that specialize in flowers for high-altitude environments. One, aptly named High Altitude Gardens, is at Ketchum, Idaho, near Sun Valley. Its catalogue is packed with wildflowers and cultivars that grow well in short-season areas. I like the honest way the catalogue presents both the rewards and the responsibilities that go with wildflower gardening, and the owners' confidence in its future. The introduction to their wildflower list reads "The '90s will be remembered as a time of landscaping naturally, cherishing the plants of the wild and bringing them into our home gardens." Their list of easy-to-grow favorites differs somewhat from Bob Heapes's; their most popular mountain wildflower is desert bluebells, *Phacelia campanularia,* and they rate the fragrant Sitka columbine, *Aquilegia formosa,* high for hummingbirds.

The Pacific Northwest

THE mild-winter belt extending from extreme northern coastal California through southern British Columbia, west of the Cascades, has such a desirable climate that wildflowers from much of North America will grow well if they are irrigated. The winters are quite wet and subject to extremely low temperatures every few years, often after a warm fall, which causes considerable damage to plants. Summers are mostly dry but not as long as those in California, and the soils are usually well drained and not strongly alkaline. Consequently, you see a greater variety of cultivated perennials than in California. As compared to California, the lowland Northwest and southwestern Canada are home to relatively few species of annual wildflowers, perhaps because the moist climate encourages a dense growth of grass and conifers that tends to crowd or shade out flowers. When it comes to perennial wildflowers, though, the upper foothills and mountains are home to a wonderfully diverse assortment, including some in the same genera found in the East. Wildflower enthusiasts in lowland gardens soon learn that they can grow these native perennials on raised beds if they incorporate grit for perfect drainage.

Water is relatively abundant and inexpensive over most of the Northwest west of the Cascades, so most gardeners feel no urgency to reduce lawn areas or to consider water conservation in their landscaping. There is no northwestern landscaping style, unless you count the incredible rhododendron gardens that grow near the ocean or the elaborate flower gardens of coastal British Columbia. Wildflowers from all over the West, except tender plants from the low desert, can be grown in this region. The Botanical Garden at the University of British Columbia at Vancouver is one of the best places to see northwestern wildflowers planted in approximations of natural habitats as well as among cultivated garden flowers.

I am told that northwesterners are perturbed about the migration of Californians into their region, but their feeling shouldn't be extended to include wildflower species native to California. If I were gardening in Medford, Salem, Portland, Seattle, or Spokane, I would want to grow meadows of California wildflowers. During my many trips to the Northwest, I have been struck by the vividness of flower colors, brought out, perhaps, by the clean, dry summer air. Why settle for the same old sweet peas and geraniums when you can have Chinese houses, *Collinsia heterophylla*; bluecurls, *Phacelia congesta*; blazing stars, *Mentzelia laevicaulis*; California bluebells, *Phacelia campanularia*; and California poppies? I can understand the impulse to plant the Oregon wildflowers that festoon the high mountain slopes — quamash, *Camassia quamash*; elephantella, *Pedicularis groenlandica*; and sulfur-flowered buckwheat,

The genus *Clarkia* has been widely hybridized and selected for a broad range of colors and unique flower forms. All clarkias are native to California except *C. pulchella*, which is spread over the Rockies. The garden flower called godetia is a *Clarkia* hybrid.

Eriogonum umbellatum, for example — but these often don't take well to the dry summer air of northwestern lowlands. Glacier lily, *Erythronium grandiflorum,* a mountain wildflower, however, will grow well in shade at lower elevations.

I would spring-plant seeds of California wildflowers in the Northwest; heavy winter rains tend to wash away seeds, and the winter annuals could be killed by severe weather. You might consider siting your wildflowers well away from your rhododendrons. Many of the California wildflowers are in shades of yellow and orange, which clash with the predominantly pink, rose, and crimson flowers of rhododendrons. (After the rhododendrons bloom, they provide a wonderful dark background for setting off flower colors.)

Northwestern gardeners with trees in their yards (except for thickly planted Douglas firs, which cast dense shade) can enjoy many more native species of woodland wildflowers than can be found elsewhere in the West. Bunchberry, *Cornus canadensis,* and redwood sorrel, *Oxalis oregana,* are happy in moist gardens along the coast; the brilliant fireweed, *Epilo-*

bium angustifolium, can withstand moderate shade; bitterroot can adapt to the Willamette Valley; mountain bluebells, with their pink-blushed, nodding flowers, love wet, partially shaded meadows; and western false Solomon's-seal, *Smilacina racemosa*, will grow almost anywhere in moist soil with plenty of organic matter. A native coastal lily, *Lilium pardalinum*, will thrive if given very well drained but continuously moist soil.

Where rainfall is heavy, dense forests of conifers shade out all but a few durable perennials and ferns. You see more species of forest-floor wildflowers among thin stands of mixed hardwoods and conifers at higher elevations. In general, eastern species of forest-floor wildflowers grow well in the Northwest, but the ones with a strong need for acid soil do best in the coastal rainbelt.

East Is East and West Is West

HAVING just said that many eastern forest-floor wildflowers will grow well in the coastal belt of the Northwest, I must add that it might not be wise to import them. The West and Northwest are already flooded with plants from elsewhere, some of which have overrun populations of native plants, especially in small and unique niches. (Recently I was told of a gardener who, in the process of restoring five acres of land in a moist valley north of Seattle to approximately its original condition, had to clear out a solid stand of reed canary grass, *Phalaris arundinacea*, an aggressive Eurasian pest.) However, I can't see any harm in shipping seeds of annual western wildflowers to the East. Their widespread use for many years apparently hasn't damaged eastern ecosystems.

Meadow seed mixtures for the West may include exotics such as baby's-breath, Shirley poppy, and cornflower as well as quick-blooming annual wildflowers such as tidy-tips.

CHAPTER 6

Wildflowers for Damp or Wet Spots

Yellow flag, which has naturalized over much of the eastern United States, prefers marshy soil.

IT'S TIME to take a fresh look at damp or wet spots in your yard or garden. Instead of trying to turn them into the ideal, well-drained soil that most cultivated plants prefer, view them as sites for wildflowers that like wet feet. So many marshes have been drained for farming or filled by developers that we must begin building new ones, even in a small way. Otherwise, we face the loss of irreplaceable plant and animal species.

Use this rule of thumb to decide whether you should consider an area to be damp: if you consistently walk around it to avoid getting your shoes muddy, it's damp. Spots that flood during heavy rains and stay damp for only a few days don't count; they can't support moisture-loving plants. Usually, damp spots don't indicate a high water table, but result from the collection of water at the surface of the soil because of underlying impervious layers of clay or hardpan. You can also find damp spots on the north or east sides of hills, near or at the bottom of the slopes, where water seeps out from higher up. During the winter in the North, damp areas on hillsides or banks tend to be covered with ice. They need not stay moist all year to support specialized wildflowers; they can go dry for a month or so during the summer.

An area is wet if water covers it much of the time. Wet spots include everything from cattail marshes and large depressions in floodplains to spring-fed seeps, peat bogs, low wet prairies, and sticky clay that is so wet that crayfish build their mud towers atop it.

Once you decide to make the most of the opportunity presented by a damp or wet spot, you have to figure out what to do with it. If it is within a typical tightly landscaped yard, it could be difficult to fit "wild wetlands" into the theme. Instead, you might want to convert the spot into a water feature such as a pool or fountain. However, if the spot is at the back of your yard, off to the side, in the woods, or on undeveloped property nearby, consider converting it into a wild wetland. We're

not talking here about a rank-smelling, mosquito-infested quagmire but about a patch of a dozen species of wonderfully different wildflowers growing in soil that smells pleasantly organic, with the puddles kept free of insects by frogs, toads, and colorful salamanders. Dragonflies chase other insects from blossom to blossom, kinds of butterflies you've never seen before suddenly appear, and marsh birds call from the tall flowers and sedges. Catalogue hype? No. Gardeners everywhere are discovering that by converting damp or wet spots into wild wetlands, they can enjoy a microcosm of the plant and animal species found naturally in marshes, ditches, and damp glens.

Preparing the Site for Planting

❧ SUNNY DAMP SPOTS

IF YOUR damp spot is out in the open, or at the most lightly shaded by trees, and is rather small, you should deepen it. Do this with care so as not to break through the layer of dense sand or packed clay that holds the water. (It usually lies a foot or two beneath the surface.) To lessen the chance of leakage, spread a thin layer of dense clay over the bottom and sides and "puddle" it by tramping on it. Dense clay layers don't hold water as well as plastic

liners, but the slow leakage helps to prevent fermentation. The finished depression should have an irregular outline and should slope gradually toward the lowest area. You will have better luck growing a wide assortment of species if you fill the depression with sand and pack it down to just below the level of the surrounding soil. Then spread a one-inch layer of moistened peat moss over the sand and mix it in to a depth of three inches. Don't mix it in deeply; excessive organic matter

Much of the native habitat of swamp milkweed has disappeared beneath waterside developments. This medium-tall pink, mauve, or occasionally white wetlands denizen will also grow in heavy garden soil. It is a host plant for monarch butterflies.

in deep, wet layers can ferment, cause odors, and create a poor growing situation.

Ideally, you should plant a meadow around a sunny damp spot, so that one environment blends with the other. However, if the spot is surrounded by mowed lawn, remove a strip of sod one foot wide around the depression, lay a sand bed, set two courses of bricks around the perimeter, and tamp them level with the surrounding turf. This will make a firm track for your lawn mower.

DAMP OR WET SPOTS IN THE WOODS

LOW-LYING shady glens and seeps call for different preparation. The best thing you can do for a glen is to mulch it with two to three inches of composted leaves mixed with sand. Seeps, which are formed by springs that either run off slowly or soak into the surrounding soil, are usually clogged with grass and layers of leaves,

Cardinal-flower grows on moist soil throughout the South and East and is valued not only for its vivid color but as a lure for hummingbirds. Selections with purple foliage are available.

which decay slowly in wet soil. Excavate the organic debris, then either make a shallow pool shaped like a basin or fill the depression with sand. You can plant the pool with some shade-tolerant aquatic wildflowers; sand-filled land will support woodland sedges, rushes, ferns, and specialized wildflowers. Either treatment will add more to your landscape than a soggy expanse of grass and fermenting leaves. Wildflower books typically describe the natural habitats of plants that like damp soils as "moist woodlands," "wet prairies," "bottomland," or "low-lying meadows," whereas wet-soil plants are usually listed with the aquatic species or described as "growing in ditches or at the water's edge."

SOIL PH AND NUTRIENT LEVELS

DAMP SPOTS tend to be acidic and poor in nutrients, and wet spots always are, except where the underlying soil is strongly alkaline or is derived from calcium-bearing rock such as diabase. Don't try to correct the acidity by adding lime or fertilizer. Most species of wildflowers that can tolerate wet feet can also tolerate acid soil, and most are also accustomed to low levels of soil fertility. Wet soil retards the conversion of fertilizers to nutrients that can be absorbed by plant roots; this is especially true of organic fertilizers, which tend to ferment. If you give your plants a good feeding with liquid fertilizer before

transplanting, that should tide them over until they build a root system that can extract nutrients dissolved in the groundwater.

PLANTING DAMP SPOTS

PLANTS are always preferable to seeds when you are planting damp spots. Woodland species grow so slowly that seeds or seedlings can be smothered by falling leaves in late autumn. (Most of these survive and spread by vegetative means as well as by seeds; nature usually provides a backup system for reproduction.) Seeds of the sun-loving species are apt to be eaten by the many birds and small mammals that are attracted to damp areas, and flooding during storms can wash the seeds away.

You can plant rather small damp spots just as you would perennial flower beds, except that you should not add fertilizer or lime. The job will go easily if your soil is sandy or loamy. However, if your soil is heavy and plastic, and if you elect not to line the spot with sand, you will find it difficult to fill in around the roots of transplants. To avoid this problem, shovel some of the clay into a wheelbarrow, let it dry for a day or two, and mix it half and half with sand. Position the wildflower plants so the crowns stand about an inch above the surrounding soil, and fill in around the roots with the soil-sand mixture. Don't tamp sticky soil; compacting it eliminates the air spaces between particles. Settle it around the roots by watering.

It's best to plant damp woodland glens in the fall, after most of the leaves have dropped. Rake the leaves aside, set the plants in place, and before bitter cold comes, mulch the plants lightly. They will set roots during early winter and spring and will probably bloom with the coming of warm weather. In contrast, spring-planted woodland wildflowers have to be nursed through the first season with frequent waterings, because they have to compete with actively growing tree roots before they are fully established.

Planting Wet Spots

LARGE marshy areas tend to refill quickly when siphoned off with a garden hose or drained with a portable pump. Planting calls for rubber boots or, after the water warms up, sneakers and shorts. If the water is more than three inches deep after you have lined the area with sand, consider piling up one or more hummocks of sandy soil to two or three inches above the water level. Many more wildflower, grass, sedge, rush, and fern species are found just above the water line than growing in the water.

It's a good idea to wait until early summer to plant marshes. The job is more pleasant then, and the warming water will encourage plants to sprout and regrow quickly.

Coping with Drought

WHEN you can clearly see the effect of drought on wetland plants, it's time to refill your wet spot to the high-water mark with a water hose. It may seem profligate to fill marshes or seeps during droughts, but if you don't, you may lose your valuable plants or, at the least, cause them to go out of bloom prematurely. Drying is more apt to occur now than before humans disturbed the landscape, because so much water runs off rather than being stored in the soil. Watch the water level, and if the soil between the plants begins to go dry, roll out the hose.

The effect of summer or fall droughts on woodland wildflowers growing in damp glens is not so apparent, and can be confused with the habit shared by many species of drying up and going dormant after the foliage canopy closes over. Droughts of three weeks or more are especially hard on freshly germinated seedlings and on wildflowers growing in a shallow layer of soil atop solid rock. Tag your woodland wildflowers so you won't forget where they are and water them every two or three weeks during dry spells by letting a hose trickle around them for about an

The tall, wild joe-pye weed species of the genus *Eupatorium* are difficult to sort out. All grow well on heavy, moist soil in full sun or afternoon shade, and bloom in late summer and fall.

hour. Don't become anxious and water more often; short dry spells are good for plants, as they force deeper rooting.

The Choice of Plants

LET ME emphasize how important it is to limit your selection of plants to species or ecotypes that grow naturally in your regional wetlands. More than any other wild area, wet spots can be overrun with exotics from other countries or from other parts of North America. For example, purple loosestrife, *Lythrum salicaria*, which originally came from Europe, has now spread from New England to the upper Midwest. It is beautiful but spreads so rapidly that it has pushed out most of the native wildflowers around lakes, marshes, ditches, and waterways. The Chinese tallow tree, *Sapium sebiferum*, commonly called the popcorn tree, has invaded marshes and creek banks from the Texas coast across to Florida. Various Australian trees, especially the *Melaleuca* species, have overgrown the Everglades. An enormous number of exotics have pushed the plants native to West Coast estuaries to near-extinction. Reed canary grass, *Phalaris arundinacea*, is overcoming the native water's-edge species around northern and northwestern ponds and lakes. If you

A tiny rock-lined pool in Virginia reflects surrounding plants of celandine poppy, green-and-gold, ferns, and garden primroses.

Marsh marigold grows along the edge of an Illinois stream, overhung by a native benzoin shrub.

are tempted to order plants from suppliers of water-garden plants, be extra careful. Although their exotic plants are fine for water gardens, where they can be controlled, they should not be planted in or near wetlands, where they can escape. The introduced tropical water hyacinth, which now clogs waterways in the deep South, is an example of an apparently innocent plant that has upset the balance of nature and is becoming an expensive-to-control nuisance.

Many woodland flowers like rich, moist soil yet can survive fairly long droughts; however, the species that are listed below for damp spots prefer a continuously high moisture content in the soil. Those listed for wet spots may grow in shallow water, at the water's edge, or in bogs or wet savannas. Some of the tender species are hardy only through zone 8; others won't tolerate hot summers. Refer to a local wildflower encyclopedia for hardiness ratings.

🙰 DAMP SPOTS

	Preferred Site		Preferred Site
Arisaema dracontium green dragon	Light shade	*Hibiscus militaris* halberd-leaved mallow	Sun
Arisaema triphyllum Jack-in-the-pulpit	Shade	*Hibiscus moscheutos* rose mallow	Sun
Caltha palustris marsh marigold	Sun	*Lobelia cardinalis* cardinal-flower	Sun or light shade
Chelone lyonii pink turtlehead	Shade	*Lysichiton americanum* skunk cabbage	Sun
Coreopsis nudata swamp coreopsis	Sun or light shade	*Mimulus ringens* Allegheny monkey-flower	Sun
Filipendula rubra queen-of-the-prairie	Sun	*Physostegia virginiana* false dragonhead	Sun or light shade
Gaultheria hispidula creeping snowberry	Shade; for northern gardens	*Rhexia virginica* meadow beauty	Sun
Gaultheria procumbens wintergreen	Shade	*Stenanthium gramineum* featherfleece	Sun; prefers boggy soil
Gentiana clausa bottle gentian	Sun, light shade	*Trollius laxus* subspp. *laxus* spreading globeflower	Sun or light shade
Geum rivale swamp avens	Sun	*Viola mcloskeyi* western sweet white violet	Light shade

	Preferred Site		Preferred Site
Acorus calamus sweet flag	Sun	**Lygopodium palmatum** creeping fern	Light shade
Aletris farinosa unicorn root	Sun	**Nelumbo lutea** yellow lotus-lily	Sun
Andromeda glaucophylla bog rosemary	Sun	**Nuphar luteum** yellow pond-lily	Sun
Asclepias incarnata swamp milkweed	Sun	**Nuphar polysepalum** western pond-lily	Sun
Bacopia caroliniana blue water-hyssop	Sun	**Nymphae odorata** hardy water-lily	Sun
Calla palustris calla lily	Light shade	**Nymphoides aquatica** floating heart	Sun
Canna flaccida golden canna	Sun or light shade	**Orontium aquaticum** golden-club, never-wet	Sun or light shade; needs shallow, running water
Cicuta maculata water hemlock	Sun		
Crinum americanum swamp lily	Sun; half-hardy	**Peltandra sagittaefolia** white arum	Sun
Dichromena latifolia whitetop sedge	Sun; half-hardy	**Polygala lutea** candyweed	Sun
Drosera species sundew	Sun	**Pontederia cordata** pickerel-weed	Sun
Eriocaulon decangulare hatpins	Sun; half-hardy	**Rorippa nasturtium-aquaticum** watercress	Sun
Helonias bullata swamp pink	Sun	**Sagittaria** species arrowhead	Sun
Hymenocallis virginiana spider-lily	Sun or light shade	**Sarracenia** species pitcher plant	Sun
Iris versicolor blue flag	Sun	**Saururus cernuus** lizard's tail	Light shade
Justica americana water-willow	Sun	**Typha latifolia** cattail	Sun
Ludwigia decurrens primrose-willow	Sun	**Utricularia juncea** horned bladderwort	Sun

Native hardy waterlily and southern blue flag transform a Mississippi pond into an aquatic landscape.

CHAPTER 7

Attracting Butterflies and Birds

A native shrub of eastern swamps, *Cephalanthus occidentalis*, provides nectar for a red admiral butterfly.

CONSIDER the plight of our native birds and butterflies. During the past half-century, as our population has nearly doubled, urban sprawl has covered fields and meadows with homes, streets, freeways, malls, industrial and office buildings, and parking lots. Farmers and developers have drained marshes, diked floodplains, and encroached on estuaries. Whole new classes of chemicals have been used to drench lawns, gardens, orchards, and turf. Even more devastating is the continuing destruction of rain forests, which have always served as winter homes for migratory birds. This tragic opera isn't over. The worst is yet to come, in the form of increased worldwide air and water pollution, which can be more destructive to the delicate systems of birds and butterflies than to humans.

Except for parklands, the densely populated areas of large cities are lost to most species of wildlife. The occasional wild bird or butterfly that visits a terrace or roof garden or a tiny landscape tucked in among city buildings is living dangerously. However, there is hope for these creatures in suburbs, small towns, and the country, if we plant wildflowers and design landscapes to meet their needs. Collectively, we should be able to grow enough plants to compensate partially for those that have been bulldozed for developments or lost to pollution. To do this, we have to develop wildlife sanctuaries not only around homes but also beside industrial buildings, in parks, on golf courses, and around schools. There is no guarantee, but if we could plant hundreds of thousands of sanctuaries, we might draw the remnants of our butterfly and bird species back into the suburbs and increase their chances for survival.

I am confident that you, like most other gardeners, are willing to make a few changes in your gardening practices in order to help in this innocent but vital crusade. But first let me refresh your memory on a few facts about birds and butterflies. True, your father and mother should have told you about such things when you were a teenager, but they may have confused you by trying to relate the needs of birds and butterflies to what humans require to survive.

Butterfly Biology

OF THE seven hundred or so species of butterflies that are native to North America, some are found as far north as Alaska, but most are found in areas with longer summers, higher humidity, and a mixture of woodland, marsh, and old-field vegetation. Some species are distributed over much of the continent; others thrive only in restricted ranges where they have found plant species and microclimates that suit them. Most butterflies are vagabonds; when you see them in your garden, they are on their way somewhere else. You could think of your wildflower garden as a rest stop on a butterfly freeway, a place where they can linger for a while, enjoy food, water, and shelter, and perhaps leave their eggs in payment.

When planting wildflowers for butterflies, you have good reasons to grow only the species or ecotypes found locally. If you introduce a wild species that is not native to your area, the plant or its seeds could contain eggs of a butterfly, moth, or other insect that is not ordinarily found where you live. If those eggs hatch, the insect can spread rapidly in the absence of the predators found in its native environment. Of course, a few non-native plants do such an extraordinary job of attracting butterflies that they deserve a place in gardens, and they have already been so widely planted that there is no danger of their bringing in new pests. These deserving plants include bloodflower, *Asclepias curassavica*; butterfly bush, *Buddleia* spp.; vervain, *Verbena bonariensis*; golden cosmos, *Cosmos sulphureus*; Mexican sunflower, *Tithonia rotundifolia*; and tartarian aster, *Aster tataricus*, a late-season nectar plant.

Every gardener has seen butterflies probing flowers and is aware that they are feeding on nectar, and most people understand the connection between caterpillars, pupae, and adult butterflies. However, fewer understand the fact that without certain host plants, butterflies will not lay eggs, for the caterpillars that hatch from them would have no food. The fertilized adult female is attracted to certain species of plants, tests them for taste or smell, and, if instinct tells her to, deposits an egg or a cluster of eggs. When these hatch, the larvae begin feeding on the host plant. Some butterfly species will lay eggs on only one plant species; others may prefer a certain kind of plant but will accept one or two others. When a caterpillar has undergone four or five instars — growth stages marked by the shedding of skin — it ceases feeding, wanders around a bit, and transforms itself into a pupa, also known as a chrysalis. Experienced butterfly watchers can identify species by their

pupae. Some are as ugly as bird dung; others are sheathed in gleaming, seemingly metallic gold or silver shells.

At one time or another, most of us have picked a pupa off a plant and tried to incubate it into a butterfly. In this stage, the insects are quiescent; you can capture them easily. We gardeners are less likely to pick off caterpillars, because they are active and have a variety of defense mechanisms, including stinging hairs and stinking "horns" that look like antlers. The parsleyworm, which is the larva of the black swallowtail butterfly, feeds on parsley-family members such as dill, fennel, carrot, Queen Anne's lace, parsley, and related plants. I've picked many a black swallowtail caterpillar off my dill and parsley, but no more. Now I plant enough for the butterflies and settle for what is left over. I always have plenty. In contrast, the familiar and much more destructive green worms that infest cabbage-family members are the larva of the non-native European cabbage butterfly. It is clearly in no danger of extinction, so I pick off the worms and feed them to our chickens, and suffer no pangs of remorse.

The beauty of wildflower gardens is that a moderate amount of damage from insects is acceptable. It's a small price to pay for the songbirds that are attracted to the bugs and beetles and to the caterpillars that grow into butterflies. Actually, relatively few butterfly caterpillars are serious garden pests, and spraying them with poisons is never wise, since the poisons can

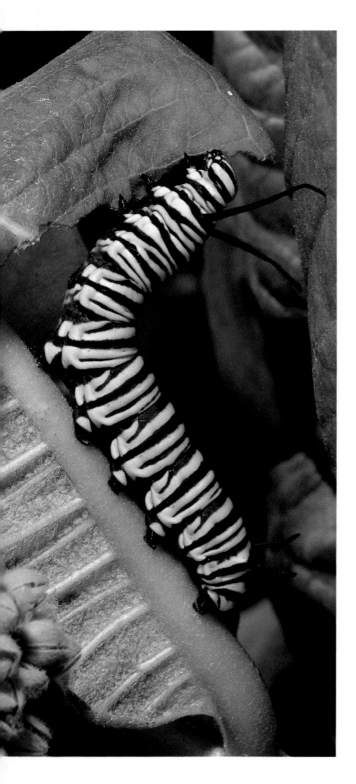

kill beneficial insects as well. In the Rocky Mountain and Pacific states, larvae of the checkerspot butterfly feed on numerous annual and perennial flowers and can disfigure them with webs, but the tradeoff for a few less-than-neat plants is a butterfly nursery. Painted lady larvae also feed on several garden flowers; their pupae seem to have been dipped in gold. The larvae of other butterfly species feed on trees, shrubs, and agricultural crops such as timber trees and clovers and are seldom seen in gardens.

By and large, the larvae of moths are much more destructive than those of butterflies. They include such notorious pests as the tomato hornworm, the gypsy moth, the armyworm, the codling moth, the oriental fruit moth, and various species that infest stored grain. Moths generally fly at night; often their larvae spin silky cocoons.

I am often asked about the longevity of butterflies, no doubt because of the publicity given to monarchs during their migrations to and from the mountains of Mexico. Monarchs may live for several months, but the individuals that fly south in the fall can be two or three generations removed from those that return to our gardens in the spring. The adults of most butterfly species do not migrate over long

A distinctive monarch caterpillar feeds on common milkweed, one of its favorite host plants. The beautiful monarch butterfly sips nectar from a goldenrod.

distances and live only one or two weeks. The eggs, pupae, or adults of many species winter over in leaf litter and standing plants, which is another argument against excessive neatness in wildflower gardens.

When you plant butterfly host and nectar plants, you may see the entire life cycles of certain butterfly species. If you are very lucky, or very patient, you may see the insects emerging from their pupae, pumping up and drying their wings, and flying away, all in a matter of an hour or so. You are more likely to see them feeding on nectar or gathering in "puddle clubs"; they often gather on areas of nutrient-rich soil to suck up the mineral broth. They love manure tea, for they are after not only the moisture but the dissolved salts and sugars. You may also see the sad side of insect life, in the tattered wings of butterfly senior citizens, soon to become food for birds or small scavengers.

Within a well-planned wildflower garden, you can provide everything butterflies need, not just to survive but to increase in numbers. In addition to host and nectar plants, butterflies need mud puddles or wet spots; they need shelter — shrubs, trees, and bushy flower plants in which they can hide from birds, find shade at midday, and rest at night; and they need stones on which to bask and build up enough body heat to fly, windbreaks to temper the wind, and masses of color to draw them from a distance.

Plantings of sun-loving wildflowers will benefit butterflies more than forest-floor wildflowers, most of which bloom before many butterfly species become active. Most butterflies prefer full sun, except at midday during hot weather, but a few species spend the bulk of their time in the shade and depend primarily on the flowers of trees, vines, and understory shrubs for nectar. If you have both sunny and shady situations, make the most of them. However, if your gardening time or budget is limited, you will draw many more species of butterflies and will be able to see them better if you plant sunny meadow flowers.

Bird Biology

MOST GARDENERS know the resident nonmigratory birds, have enjoyed their songs, and have seen their nests and the tense situations that arise when the babies are ready to leave the nest. Birders love the winter residents but eagerly anticipate the return of the robins, orioles, thrushes, warblers, hummingbirds, and other common migratory species, rejoicing in this annual sign of winter's end. We know how to attract and feed the more common species and have done a pretty good job of it. However, we can do a better job on their behalf and we can serve the less common species as well if we will learn just a bit more about their habits.

It is important to know that some bird species are basically insectivorous and some are basically seed-eaters. Many species are opportunistic and will eat anything they can catch or glean, animal or vegetable. Some, like the woodpeckers, cuckoos, flickers, and creepers, dig insects out of tree bark or wood. Cuckoos and a few other kinds of birds capture tent caterpillars in or near their webbed nests. Others, like the warblers, inspect each tree or shrub twig and blossom for insects. Still others, like robins and the introduced starlings, search for worms and grubs in the ground. A few, like swifts, swallows, and purple martins, capture insects on the wing. But across the board, the majority of bird species visit wildflowers to feed on insects and spiders, and later on dried seeds.

Seed-eaters and insectivorous birds alike benefit from plantings of wildflowers. Some birds are drawn by the crop of bugs and spiders, others by the flowers' buds and seeds. Large drifts of wildflowers attract more birds than small patches or individual plants, and the greater the range of plant species, the greater the likelihood that you will attract uncommon birds.

Most of us provide water and food for birds during the winter and continue sup-

Birds will strip this elderberry of its juicy purple-black fruits soon after they ripen.

plying water throughout the year. (Actually, we should continue feeding birds during the spring nesting period rather than closing their breadline abruptly at the end of winter.) Many of us put up nests for bug-eating species such as wrens, bluebirds, and purple martins, but birds also need shelter, nesting sites, and way stations where they can perch temporarily en route to the feeder or the wildflower garden. All of these needs can be provided with native trees and shrubs placed strategically around the garden. Tall flowers within your sunny wildflower garden or meadow can also serve some of the same purposes as shrubs; sunflower, mallow, and hibiscus species are examples.

Attracting Hummingbirds

HUMMINGBIRDS are delightful creatures — audacious, acrobatic, endearing little showoffs. Most gardeners are thrilled just to have one occasionally visit their garden. Yet by planting selected wildflowers, you can help reverse the decline in numbers of hummingbirds by attracting nesting pairs. And by planting separate patches of hummingbirds' favorite wildflowers in your front, side, and back yards, you can also keep these fiercely territorial little birds from driving off other hummers.

Hummingbirds need the balanced diet they can get from flower nectar and from insects and spiders that crawl in or on the blossoms. Be sure to include tubular flowers that are especially rich in nectar and easy for hummingbirds to probe, and some blossoms that are either pendent or tilted downward to discourage bees and other insects that compete for nectar.

The rewards are worth the effort. West Coast and southwestern gardeners can enjoy fifteen hummingbird species, some of which are seen only along the Mexican border or in isolated canyons. The mountain states are home to black-chinned and broad-tailed hummingbirds. The rest of the country has to settle for three species: the widely adapted ruby-throated hummingbird; as a nonbreeding visitor along the western Gulf coast, the buff-bellied hummingbird; and, once in a blue moon for eastern birders, wandering rufous hummingbirds that have strayed from their northwestern home. Only a few areas of the country, all in the Midwest, are without hummingbirds, and only the birds know the reason.

Hummingbirds can consume half their weight in nectar every day, so you need to plant lots of flowers to provide enough food to keep them from moving on. If you have only a small wildflower area, or if it lacks water or the shrubs and small trees these birds need for perching, you may need to put up feeders. If you have a sizable meadow in which wildflowers bloom from spring through fall, if you have shrubs and trees nearby, and if you keep water handy, you have a good chance of

attracting a nesting pair. Those who don't have a meadow but grow large perennial borders can interplant special hummingbird flowers among the perennials; all are showy enough to hold their own with cultivars.

Hummingbirds are essentially summer residents, but of course linger on where winters are rather short and mild. You cannot influence the departure and arrival dates of hummingbirds migrating to or from Mexico and Central America by feed-

Native wildflowers include many vines. One of the most beautiful (and attractive to hummingbirds) is coral honeysuckle. (I was too busy working on this book to build a trellis, so my wife made one of metal fenceposts and alder branches.)

ing; they come and go when they are ready. You can, however, make sure that they have plenty to eat by planting early, mid-season, and late-blooming wildflowers known to be popular food sources. To attract more hummingbirds, keep fresh

water in your birdbath and put a few flat stones in it to give these hygienic little birds the shallow water they love.

When it comes to selecting hummingbird flowers for your garden, emphasize red and orange-yellow. The birds can see red, but the competing bees can't distinguish red from any other dark color. Among the red or orange tubular wildflowers known to attract ruby-throated hummingbirds are cardinal-flower, *Lobelia cardinalis*; tropical sage, *Salvia coccinea*; trumpet honeysuckle, *Lonicera sempervirens*; Indian pink, *Spigelia marilandica*; bee balm and bergamot, *Monarda didyma* and *M. fistulosa*; Texas plume, *Ipomopsis rubra*; trumpet creeper, *Campsis radicans*; cross-vine, *Bignonia capriolata*;

Vernonia noveboracensis, an ironweed, attracts a swallowtail butterfly to its nectar receptacles.

stone, bleeding heart, *Dicentra* spp. For late bloom try the small-flowered red morning-glory, *Ipomoea coccinea*; *Hibiscus* of several species; the half-hardy turk's cap, *Malvaviscus aboreus*; evening primrose, *Oenothera biennis*; and the naturalized *Verbena bonariensis*.

Californian and southwestern gardeners can plant Arizona trumpet, *Epilobium canum* subspp. *latifolium* (= *Zauschneria latifolia*); scarlet delphinium, *Delphinium cardinale*; Texas plume; and many of the native penstemons, monkey-flowers, and sages. Many western flowers have evolved to attract hummingbirds, far more than in the East.

Nature arranged for different flowers to attract the hummingbirds and butterflies, probably to reduce competition. Only a few do all things for all creatures. Therefore, to have an all-purpose wildflower meadow or garden, you need to include flowers especially selected for hummingbirds, butterflies, and seed-eating birds. By scanning books on the wildflowers of your state — books with color illustrations — you can quickly select sun-loving species with red or orange tubular flowers to attract hummingbirds and flowers of the composite family, with blossoms like daisies or sunflowers, to provide landing pads for butterflies. I rate the tropical sage, *Salvia coccinea*, very high for feeding hummingbirds, butterflies, and seed-eating birds, and expect to see other red-flowered salvias introduced by wildflower nurseries to join the garden favorites au-

and spotted jewelweed, *Impatiens capensis*. For early bloom, try birdfoot violet, *Viola pedata*; columbine, *Aquilegia* spp.; wild sweet William, *Phlox maculata* or *P. divaricata*; and if your soil overlies lime-

tumn sage, *S. greggii*, and scarlet sage, *S. splendens.* You will doubtless develop your own list of hummingbird plants as you watch the feeding habits of these speedy fliers. (While I am writing this, only a few early-blooming red flowers are open in my wildflower meadow, and hummingbirds have been feeding from them since their arrival three weeks ago. But as if to show that they are not all that particular about flower colors, one just circled each of a dozen spires of white *Penstemon digitalis*, dipping into each floret.)

The Compatibility of Birds and Butterflies

IT BOTHERS some gardeners to see the occasional butterfly taken on the wing or driven to the ground by an insectivorous bird. There is no doubt that butterflies and caterpillars form a large part of the diet of songbirds, but you must understand that nature makes allowances for this. Those butterfly species that are not equipped with alarm colorations, startling displays, or a foul taste are good at laying and hiding many eggs; they multiply rapidly. If you plant a garden to attract and feed butterflies, songbirds will be drawn to it. Except when feeding their young, the majority will eat seeds and buds in preference to insects, and the insect-eaters will fill some of their need for protein by eating

beetles, moths, and their grubs and larvae as well as butterflies. It all balances out; your wildflowers feed butterflies and other insects, and they in turn feed insectivorous birds. Your entire garden will benefit; the birds drawn to your wildflowers will glean the insects from your cultivated annuals, perennials, trees, shrubs, and vegetables.

Adapting Your Garden to Wildlife

I CAN think of no other gardening goal that will bring you more rewards with less effort and expense than designing a garden and selecting plants to favor wildlife. You don't have to take it on blind faith; you have already seen that birds and butterflies are occasionally drawn to gardens designed purely for human pleasure or as settings for homes. But you may not realize that mowed lawns, sheared shrubs, and neatly raked beds fail as wildlife magnets; most are inhospitable deserts to birds and butterflies. If you want to go all the way toward attracting and supporting these creatures, you may have to change three aspects of your garden: its design, its maintenance, and the choice of plants.

Let's assume that you have a sunny area for a vegetable and herb garden and a perennial border in your back yard. There is no need to change it substantially. However, you do need a few groups of shrubs or small trees at the rear of your garden or along the sides, to serve as lookout points and nesting sites for birds and as host plants for butterfly larvae. Locate points along buildings or fences where you can train flowering, climbing vines that attract hummingbirds — native honeysuckle, trumpet creeper, and such. From a design standpoint, that's really all the modification your back yard needs, unless you can find the space to fit a birdbath into the plan.

It's the front yard that usually needs the help. If your front yard is mostly or totally shaded, you will find it difficult to upgrade to wildlife standards, because root competition will make it hard to establish an understory of shrubs and flowers that feed birds and butterflies. It's difficult, but not impossible: if you set durable concrete containers in sun-dappled spots, you can plant them with summer-blooming flowers that tolerate shade. Set the containers on bricks to keep tree roots from invading them through the drainage holes. If your front yard is sunny, you can integrate it with the back yard to form one large wildlife sanctuary. Fences and gates mean nothing to birds and butterflies.

Many contemporary landscapes are self-defeating; they don't draw the full spectrum of prey and predator. When they attract injurious insects, there are few birds and predatory insects to feed on them. Further, if we had done it deliberately, we could not have designed a worse scenario for the survival of wildlife. In contemporary landscapes, the emphasis is on manicured lawns and broad-leaved evergreens or conifers that are green most of the year. Conifers provide shelter and seeds but none of the color and nectar that attract and support butterfly and bird life. Flowering shrubs, especially those that set berries after blossoming, are more valuable for wildlife. Borders of run-of-the-mill cultivated perennials usually include some good butterfly and bird flowers, but you can make them more effective by careful choice of cultivars. Generally, double-flowered cultivars of perennials with tightly bunched, frilled, or convoluted petals are less attractive than single-flowered cultivars as nectar sources, because access is more difficult.

You should be relieved to learn that the major change you need to make in maintaining your garden is to do less of it. Do less raking of leaves and small branches. Allow the frozen frames of wildflowers, perennials, and garden annuals to stand through the winter. If you see butterfly larvae feeding on a weed, let it stay; don't pull it up. If you notice that birds like to feed on the seeds of certain weeds and grasses, let them stand. By definition, a weed is "a plant out of place," so if it serves a useful purpose, give it a place in your garden as a wildlife food plant. Many species of butterflies overwinter beneath leaf litter or snug within clumps of frozen perennials and grasses. If you rake away litter or tidy up your garden before spring, you can do considerable harm to the butterfly population. If you can, delay turning over the soil in vegetable and flower beds until spring to reduce damage to those butterfly species that pupate just beneath the surface.

Designing a Garden and Selecting Plants for Butterflies

CERTAIN varieties of garden flowers and herbs have long been famous as butterfly nectar plants: butterfly bush, yellow cosmos, lantana, verbena, marigold, and garlic chives, to name a few. Yet for every exotic flower that serves as a host plant or nectar source, there are several native North American species that will do as well or better. The problem is that only in recent years have naturalists begun logging the numbers and kinds of butterflies drawn to gardens planted partly or solely with wildflowers. They know most of the host and nectar plants preferred in the wild but are still learning what butterflies will choose when served a smorgasbord of species planted close together. (As a class, it is hard to beat the prairie wildflowers as nectar plants.)

One factor, however, does need to be considered when you are choosing wildflowers for your butterfly garden — the provision of host plants. If you have a small garden, you won't have room for many host plants, and you'll probably have none of the trees and shrubs that feed certain butterfly larvae. You can plant *Asclepias* species to feed the monarchs — not just butterfly weed, *A. tuberosa*, but also the milkweeds and the West Indian native bloodflower, *A. curassavica*. You can also plant members of the carrot or parsley family to feed the larvae of black swallowtails. You don't have to settle for parsley, dill, carrots, or their invasive relative, Queen Anne's lace. Some of the native wildflowers in this family are alexanders, *Angelica atropurpurea*; rattlesnake-master, *Eryngium yuccifolium*; and meadow-parsnip, *Zizia aptera*, which is shade-tolerant. The caterpillars of some species, such as the sulfurs, feed on legumes; their needs can be met by the native lupines, baptisias, cassias, lespedezas, and vetches. The wild buckwheats, *Eriogonum* spp., feed the caterpillars of several western butterflies. Some of the fritillaries feed on violets but will switch to passionflowers during the summer. The caterpillars of crescents are found on wild asters, and those of painted ladies on composite or daisy-family members. Plant grasses and sedges to feed caterpillars of ringlets, wood nymphs, and many skippers.

Identifying butterflies is part of the fun. The common species can be recognized from a distance, but many butterflies will let you come close enough to check the colors and patterns on their upper and lower wing surfaces. The small, restless butterflies called skippers are more difficult; they are constantly on the move. Skippers are often confused with moths,

but you can tell them by their antennae: skippers usually have threadlike antennae with knobs or hooks on the end, whereas the antennae of moths look more like feathers or combs. The simple pocket-size butterfly books usually include color photos showing butterflies with their wings open and closed.

Naturalists have found that wildflowers planted in drifts in the sun draw the most butterflies. These insects are attracted by color and fragrance, and they are more strongly drawn to big, bold splashes of

A great spangled fritillary finds that the disk flowers of purple prairie coneflower make a good landing pad from which to feed.

color and concentrations of fragrance. Butterflies like two kinds of flowers most: clusters of nectar-filled tubular blossoms that they can probe in sequence, and large, rather flat blossoms that provide them with landing pads. Purple, red, orange, and yellow attract the most species; blue and white flowers are less popular. However, color preferences can vary from species to species, so you should plant the entire color palette.

On a windy day, butterflies will move to the lee side of tall plants or to flowers protected by dense evergreens or buildings. They have more important things to do than battle strong breezes. During very hot days, they will seek the shade cast by trees, shrubs, and large wildflower plants, and they hide among these same plants to escape from birds.

Especially valuable for butterflies are early-blooming flowers that are open when the first hatches emerge or the first returning migrants arrive, and the late-blooming species that are still in bloom after the first fall frosts. Early violets are occasionally weighed down with butterflies, as are late-blooming asters and joe-pye weed. Many butterfly species are incredibly hardy, but you can help them through perilous times by planting for very early and late bloom. Certain native shrubs and vines bloom very early; others have juicy fruit that draws hordes of butterflies after it has been frozen by fall frosts and thawed by the sun. Although sun-loving meadow flowers do the most good for butterflies, you should provide some of the woodland wildflowers as well; they tend to bloom earlier, and in fact might be the only flowers in bloom when the butterflies arrive. Mixing exotic garden flowers and wildflowers in your butterfly-and-bird garden often leads to good results. You can arrange them in the usual fashion of perennial and annual borders, by height, color, texture, and season of bloom, but I think that drifts of at least three to five plants of several species, arranged as they would occur naturally in a meadow, work best.

The staff at Callaway Gardens, in Pine Mountain, Georgia, where many *Victory Garden* programs are taped for the Public Broadcasting Corporation, have found several wildflowers to be effective nectar sources for butterflies: Stokes' aster, *Stokesia laevis*; moss verbena, *Verbena tenuisecta*; purple coneflower, *Echinacea purpurea*; butterfly weed; joe-pye weed, *Eupatorium* spp.; and white horsemint, *Pycnanthemum incanum*. For host plants they grow maypop and passionflower, *Passiflora caerula* and *P. incarnata*; dutchman's pipe, *Aristolochia durior*; red bay, *Persea borbonia*; and many species of wild violets and partridge-peas, *Cassia* spp. Their butterfly gardens are a merry mixture of garden flowers and wildflowers from all over the country.

Designing a Wildflower Garden for Birds

WILDFLOWERS draw insects of many kinds to their nectar, far more than conventional landscapes do. In turn, the concentration of insects attracts a wide variety of insectivorous birds and, during the nesting season, seed-eating birds that feed their young with insects. The dense cover provided by tall, thickety wildflowers shelters seed-eaters. Toward the end of the growing season, when flower seed heads begin to mature, the seed-eaters predominate.

I doubt if your choice of wildflower species will have a significant effect on the number of insectivorous birds drawn to your garden or meadow. Continuous bloom from early, midseason, and late species will keep them coming, as will shrubs and small trees planted nearby for perching, shelter, and nesting, and water for drinking and bathing. But your choice of species can be most important in feeding seed-eating songbirds during the fall and winter; they like variety in their diet. The single-flowered members of the composite family, such as cosmos, attract finches and other seed-eaters. Flowers of composites can be flat, like daisies or sunflowers, or bunched together in tufts, like goldenrod, thistles, or ironweed. Less obvious is the attraction of species that set their seeds in bottle- or vaselike ovaries along their stems: the salvias, penstemons, evening primroses, and phlox. When I set a feeder in the middle of a small meadow this past winter, it drew hordes of birds, but I do believe the juncos and sparrows spent as much time gleaning seeds among the frozen plants of tropical sage as they did around the base of the feeder.

Everyone has seen how fond finches are of the seeds of composites of every kind, from the large-flowered sunflowers down to the small-flowered asters and coreopsis. These birds are not ground-feeders by choice, so they look for flowers that provide perches for feeding. The ground-feeders, in contrast — sparrows, juncos, towhees, and the large seed-eaters like cardinals that are too heavy to perch on flower stems — love to scratch and peck around wildflowers with seed pods that burst and scatter their contents. They will occasionally flutter up to low branches and ride them down to get at seed pods that are just out of reach. Some of the most prolific seeders are the tropical sages, evening primroses, *Coreopsis* spp., *Gaillardia* spp., *Penstemon* spp., mustard-family members, grasses, and the mallows. Don't forget that while fall and winter food from seed heads is most often emphasized, most songbirds also appreciate fresh berries and the protein provided by insects and spiders drawn to wildflowers during the summer. Nesting birds in particular need an abundant supply of caterpillars and adult insects to feed their young. If you want birds on your property, make it possible for them to feed their young without long foraging flights. They don't like long commutes any more than we do!

How many bird species your garden will attract depends on some factors beyond your control: its proximity to a flyway for migratory species; whether it is surrounded by city, suburbs, or country; its nearness to a wide range of large tree species, marshes, or bodies of water; and the length of time it has been in place. Trying to predict how effective it will be as a magnet for birds is useless. You can lay out a wildflower feast for the birds, as most people do, and hope that the word gets out that you are throwing a nonstop party for them. You may get lucky, but then again, you may see mostly black-birds, starlings, house finches, cowbirds, and jays. Often the single most important thing you can do is to set up a little foun-tain-birdbath combination. Birds love fresh water, and instinct tells them that moving water means fresh water. Give them moving water and keep trying, and one day a flash of orange, scarlet, or blue plumage may send you scurrying for the binoculars.

SHELTERBELTS FOR BIRDS

ONE GOOD way to attract birds is to grow fruits and berries to feed them while providing much-needed shelterbelts or hedgerows where they can take cover from wind, rain, cold, and predators. Shel-terbelts take up so much room that they are not practical for average-size gardens, but you can plant them on vacant lots and spacious suburban and country prop-erties. What not to plant is an important consideration. You should avoid stoloni-ferous bushes such as multiflora roses,

Just before frost, aster and goldenrod species and Indian grass provide much-needed nectar for migrating butterflies and those that overwinter as pupae. The tall plants, rich with seeds, will shelter and feed wild birds throughout the winter.

which form spreading thickets, and invasive plants that root wherever their arching stems touch the ground. Ideally, a shelterbelt should include small trees, large shrubs, shrub roses, and vines, and a border of tall, robust wildflowers on the side away from the prevailing wind.

From watching birds on my farm, I know that *Juniperus virginiana* forms a good basis for a shelterbelt. Other erect juniper, fir, and spruce species grow farther north and west. On cold winter evenings I can see flocks of birds funneling into the dense cedars, and in June and July, when the juniper berries are ripe, birds come from all over to feast on them.

For giving birds protection from cats, I can think of no better plant than the ferociously armed non-native hardy orange, *Poncirus trifoliata*, which is reliably winter-hardy through zone 7. Farther north the spiny hawthorns should provide a deterrent. Were it not for its susceptibility to fire blight, the old-fashioned tall and prickly firethorn, *Pyracantha coccinea*, would be ideal to provide protection along with attractive berries. Serviceberry, *Amelanchier* spp., lacks thorns but packs on plenty of small purple-black fruit. In cooler climates the native mountain ash, *Sorbus* spp., grows into a small, heavily berried tree. Native wild grapes, Virginia creeper, elderberries, and viburnums set fruit in late summer, well before plants with firmer berries, such as the hollies, which require freezing to make the fruit edible.

The lee side of hedgerows is a great place for those wildflowers that are too large for most gardens. Giant sunflower, *Helianthus giganteus*; wild sunflower, *H. annuus*; Maximilian sunflower, *H. maximiliani*; tall coreopsis, *Coreopsis tripteris*; tickseed-sunflower, *Bidens aristosa*; cup plant, *Silphium perfoliatum*; and prairie dock, *Silphium terebinthinaceum*, are all heavy seed producers and should draw hummingbirds and butterflies as well.

Books on wildlife habitats recommend planting blackberries, gooseberries, currants, and other familiar garden berries among hedgerows. However, I would not recommend it if you grow the same berries in your garden or orchard, since birds drawn to the hedgerow plantings would simply move on to the garden. You can, however, protect your garden berries by draping the bushes with the new metallic bird-alarm flash tape, which is red on one side and silver on the other; early trials are very encouraging.

Please, Don't Spray

COMMON sense will tell you not to spray your wildflowers with toxic insecticides, which will kill not only the target insects but the beautiful and beneficial insects as well. What you may not know is that the widely used biological insecticide *Bacillus thuringiensis*, often called simply BT, will kill the larvae of butterflies and beneficial wasps as well as green worms on cabbage-family members. Toxic insecticides are most often used on specialty plants that attract a number of insects: roses and fruit and nut trees, for example. *Bacillus thuringiensis* is most often used on leafy vegetables. If you grow and spray these crops, keep them well away from your wildflower garden to minimize damage to butterflies and beneficial insects.

Wildflowers seldom suffer much insect damage, and when they do, it is usually from butterfly larvae, such as monarch caterpillars on milkweed-family members like butterfly weed. You can accept such damage because you know the rewards. However, if you see "hot spots" of aphids or spider mites beginning to develop in your wildflowers, you may be inclined to reach for the sprayer. If you do, use insecticidal soap, or the still-experimental emulsions of vegetable oil and detergent, but only on the affected plants. Garlic water, made by crushing and sieving garlic cloves into water, is effective against flying insects. Spray your plants in early morning, before the butterflies begin to fly. I use different means of controlling insect and disease hot spots on perennial wildflowers. In my garden, blue stars, *Amsonia tabernaemontana,* suffers severe damage from spider mites during hot, dry weather. I cut the tops back and burn them. Come fall, new, clean foliage regrows from the roots. I also thin out thick stands of bee balm to reduce the severity of mildew. (Thinning improves air circulation between plants.)

Stop and think before you spray any plant in your wildflower garden, even with insecticidal soap. I can remember reading on the label that an insecticidal soap wouldn't harm ladybugs, so I sprayed a patch of plants that were being disfigured by leafhoppers. The soap killed the leafhoppers and didn't kill the adult ladybugs, but I was dismayed to see that it did kill the soft-bodied ladybug larvae right and left. That taught me to be more patient — to give the leafhoppers time to move on, and to accept a bit of damage. Tolerance for insect damage is directly proportional to the distance between you and the troubled plants; if insect damage bothers you, back off and focus on the panorama rather than on the problem.

Refraining from spraying makes you feel good, too. Watching a hummingbird making its morning rounds from the still-open evening primroses to the just-opening tropical sage, and then to the bergamot and the vervain, is so rewarding when you know you have not contaminated your flowers' nectar with insecticides. Then, when you experience the sheer delight of discovering a hummingbird nest in one of your shrubs, you will commit yourself more than ever to keeping your microecosystem free from toxic chemicals.

For more information on wildlife habitats for home grounds and for prices of books about attracting wild birds and butterflies, contact the National Wildlife Federation, 1400 Sixteenth Street, Washington, D.C. 20036–2266.

Jack-in-the-pulpit, or Indian turnip, naturalizes quickly in moist, acid woodland soil. The color of the hood, or spadix, can vary from green to striped.

CHAPTER 8

Regional Plant Lists

Choice Wildflowers for New England[1]

THIS LIST is based in part on information from the New England Wild Flower Society. The usual flower color(s) of each wild species is listed beneath the common name.

SHADY SITES

	Preferred Soil pH	Preferred Site
Arisaema triphyllum Jack-in-the-pulpit The hood can be green or striped with brown.	Strongly acid	Moist, well drained

---

[1]Some of the sun-loving wildflowers listed are native to other parts of the United States but grow well in New England. Because New England was originally heavily forested, more woodland species than meadow wildflowers are native to the area. So many ferns are native or adapted to New England that I have made no attempt to recommend species.

	Preferred Soil pH	Preferred Site
Asarum canadense wild ginger brownish purple	Mildly acid; likes calcium[2]	Moist, well drained
Cimicifuga racemosa black cohosh white spires	Mildly acid	Moist, well drained; light shade
Clintonia borealis bluebead lily greenish yellow, dark blue fruit	Strongly acid	Moist, well drained
Cypripedium calceolus var. **pubescens** yellow lady's-slipper yellow marked with purple-brown	Alkaline	Moist, well drained; light shade
Dicentra canadensis squirrel corn greenish white; and **D. cucullaria** Dutchman's breeches white to creamy yellow	Weakly acid; likes calcium	Moist, well drained; open woods
Dodecatheon meadia shooting star magenta, lavender, white	Neutral to slightly acid; likes calcium	Moist, well drained
Erythronium americanum yellow trout-lily often dark-spotted	Weakly acid	Low-lying, moist
Galax urceolata galax white, small	Strongly acid	Moist, well drained; marginally hardy
Goodyera pubescens downy rattlesnake-plantain white, small	Weakly to strongly acid	Dry, well drained

[2]Certain plants require acid soil but respond to applications of calcium. In their wild habitats, the soil is derived from calcium-bearing rock, which, despite acidity, provides sufficient calcium to meet the plants' requirements for cell-building and metabolic processes. The acidity makes certain micronutrients more available than they would be in neutral soils.

Hepatica acutiloba sharp-lobed hepatica pale bluish white	Neutral to slightly acid; likes calcium	Moist, well drained
Iris cristata crested iris blue with white or yellow crest, often spotted	Moderately to strongly acid	Moist, well drained; light shade
Lilium philadelphicum wood lily orange to orange-red with purple spots	Strongly acid	Dry, sandy soil; sun or light shade
Lilium superbum turk's-cap lily orange-scarlet with purple-brown spots	Strongly acid	Moist, peaty soil
Maianthemum canadense false lily-of-the-valley white with pale red fruit	Mildly acid	Moist, well drained
Mertensia virginica Virginia bluebells purplish blue with pink blush	Moderately acid; likes calcium	Moist, well drained; light shade
Mitchella repens partridgeberry white with red berries	Strongly acid	Moist, well drained
Polemonium reptans Jacob's ladder blue	Mildly acid	Moist, well drained
Polygonatum commutatum **(= P. biflorum)** great Solomon's-seal greenish white	Mildly acid	Moist, well drained
Sanguinaria canadensis bloodroot white, occasionally tinged with pink	Neutral to slightly acid	Moist, well drained; light shade
Tiarella cordifolia foamflower white, occasionally tinged with red	Moderately acid	Moist, well drained

	Preferred Soil pH	Preferred Site
Trientalis borealis starflower white, small	Mildly acid	Moist, well drained
Trillium erectum wakerobin brownish purple	Weakly to moderately acid; likes calcium	Moist, well drained
Trillium grandiflorum white trillium white, fading to pink or rose	Weakly acid; likes calcium	Moist, well drained
Trillium undulatum painted trillium white marked with red chevrons	Moderately to strongly acid	Quite moist, humusy soil
Uvularia perfoliata wood merrybells yellow	Mildly acid	Rich, moist soil
Viola rostrata long-spurred violet lilac with dark spots	Neutral	Rich, moist soil

❦ SUNNY SITES

	Preferred Soil pH	Preferred Site
Anemone patens (= Pulsatilla patens) pasqueflower (naturalized) blue-violet	Adaptable	Well drained
Aquilegia canadensis American columbine red/yellow	Neutral to slightly acid	Moist, well drained
Asclepias incarnata swamp milkweed rose-pink, occasionally white	Moderately to strongly acid	Moist to wet
Aster laevis smooth aster blue or pale purple	Slightly acid	Moist
Aster linariifolius bristly aster violet-blue	Strongly acid	Well drained

The petals of *Trillium grandiflorum* turn pink with age. This species is widely distributed but scarce in some areas because of heavy collecting. It is slow-growing and difficult to transplant.

Aster spectabilis showy aster violet-purple	Moderately to strongly acid	Dry
Baptisia australis blue false indigo indigo blue	Slightly acid	Moist; marginally hardy
Boltonia asteroides boltonia white, blue, purple	Moderately to strongly acid	Moist; marginally hardy

	Preferred Soil pH	Preferred Site
Calla palustris wild calla green/white spathe with red berries	Strongly acid	Shallow water
Cassia hebecarpa wild senna yellow	Mildly acid	Moist
Coreopsis auriculata dwarf tickseed or eared coreopsis deep golden-yellow petals and disks	Mildly acid	Moist, well drained; marginally hardy
Eupatorium rugosum **(= E. urticifolium)** snow thoroughwort white	Mildly acid	Moist, well drained
Filipendula rubra queen-of-the-prairie deep pink to purple-red	Mildly acid	Moist
Gentiana andrewsii closed gentian blue, aging to purple	Neutral	Moist to wet; light shade
Gentiana autumnalis pine barrens gentian yellow/blue with spots	Strongly acid	Moist, sandy
Geranium maculatum wild geranium rose-purple	Strongly acid	Moist, well drained; light shade
Heterotheca mariana **(= Chrysopsis mariana)** Maryland goldenaster yellow	Moderately acid	Dry
Hypericum buckleyi St. Johnswort (sub-shrub) yellow	Mildly acid	Moist, well drained
Hypoxis hirsuta yellow stargrass bright yellow	Strongly acid	Moist, well drained
Lewisia tweedyi lewisia salmon-pink, large	Mildly acid	Sandy, well drained

Liatris punctata dwarf blazing star pinkish purple with spots	Adaptable	Moist, well drained
Lilium canadense Canada lily orange-yellow to red with spots	Strongly acid to neutral	Moist, well drained; woodland edge
Marshallia grandiflora Barbara's buttons pink, purple, white	Moderately acid	Moist, well drained
Mimulus ringens Allegheny monkey-flower blue to violet-blue, occasionally pink or white	Strongly acid	Water's edge
Penstemon hirsutus hairy beard-tongue purplish violet	Mildly acid	Moist, well drained
Phlox ovata mountain phlox purple, pink, occasionally white	Adaptable	Moist, well drained
Potentilla tridentata cinquefoil white	Strongly acid	Moist
Senecio aureus golden ragwort yellow	Mildly acid	Moist
Solidago flexicaulis zigzag goldenrod yellow	Mildly acid	Moist
Thalictrum pubescens *(= T. polygamum)* tall meadow-rue white	Mildly acid	Constantly moist, well drained; woodland edge
Trollius laxus subsp. *laxus* spreading globeflower greenish yellow	Neutral to slightly acid	Moist to wet; light shade
Verbesina alternifolia wingstem yellow	Mildly acid	Moist

This Mississippi garden combines Stokes' aster with yellow sundrops, pink milfoil, and a white selection from *Phlox paniculata.*

Southeastern Wildflowers, Grasses, and Ferns

FIVE EXPERIENCED wildflower gardeners cooperated with me in developing this list of wildflowers, grasses, and ferns adapted to the Southeast. Most species are native to the region, but a few are from the prairie states, the Northeast, or the Southwest. Certain species may prove a bit tender at mountain elevations, and a few woodland species from the mountains may need additional water in dry Piedmont or lowland gardens. However, overall, the plants on this list should grow well from eastern Texas roughly through southeastern Pennsylvania.

WILDFLOWERS

	Preferred Site
Actaea pachypoda (= A. alba) white baneberry white berries	Woodland; a mountain plant
Amorpha fruticosa (= A. tennessensis) false indigo blue, white, or purple spikes	Full sun
Amsonia hubrichtii blue star light blue	Full sun or afternoon shade
Anemone lancifolia windflower white	Woodland
Anemonella thalictroides rue-anemone white to pale purple-pink	Woodland
Angelica venenosa woodland angelica white	Woodland
Aquilegia canadensis wild columbine red and yellow (bicolor)	Afternoon shade

	Preferred Site
Arisaema dracontium green dragon green hood and creamy white flower	Woodland; a wetlands plant
Arisaema triphyllum Jack-in-the-pulpit green or striped brown hood	Woodland; likes moist soil
Arnica acaulis leopard's-bane yellow	Full sun
Aruncus dioicus goatsbeard white	Afternoon shade or woodland; a mountain plant, needs moist soil when grown in the lowlands
Asarum canadense wild ginger brownish purple flowers hidden under foliage	Woodland; likes lime
Asclepias tuberosa butterfly weed red, yellow, orange	Full sun

Aster species, including
   A. dumosus, bushy aster; white, blue, lavender
   A. linariifolius, stiff aster; blue, violet, near pink, or white
   A. novae-angliae, New England aster; violet with yellow center, occasionally pink or white; many cultivars available
   A. paludosus, large-flowered aster; blue, violet
   A. pilosus, frost aster; white, rarely pink
   A. spectabilis, showy aster; blue to violet
	Full sun

Baptisia species, including
   B. alba, wild white indigo
   B. australis, wild blue indigo
   B. bracteata, wild cream indigo
   B. lanceolata, pineland indigo; yellow
	Full sun or afternoon shade

Bidens aristosa and related species tickseed-sunflower yellow	Full sun

Calamintha georgiana (= Satureja georgiana)
Georgia savory
white, occasionally pink or lavender

Full sun or
afternoon shade

Callirhoe papaver
winecups
magenta, occasionally white

Full sun or
afternoon shade

Chamaelirium luteum
fairy-wand
white

Woodland

Chelone glabra (white, pink, rose-purple)
and **C. obliqua** (purple, white)
snakehead or turtlehead

Woodland or
afternoon shade;
wetlands plants

Chimaphila maculata
spotted wintergreen
white with variegated foliage

Woodland

Chrysogonum virginianum
green-and-gold
a variable species; yellow petals, sometimes notched

Afternoon shade
or woodland

Cimicifuga racemosa
black cohosh
white

Woodland

Claytonia virginica
spring beauty
white to pink

Woodland or
afternoon shade

Conradina verticillata
Cumberland rosemary
lavender-pink

Full sun

Conradina canescens
(from northern Florida)
bluish white; blue-green foliage

Full sun

Coreopsis species, including
   C. auriculata, eared coreopsis
   C. integrifolia, chipola coreopsis
   C. lanceolata (= C. grandiflora),
   lance-leaved coreopsis
   C. major, whorled-leaf coreopsis
All coreopsis have yellow flowers.

Full sun or
afternoon shade

Crinum americanum
swamp crinum
pink to white

Full sun or
afternoon shade;
winter-hardy only
in the Deep South

	Preferred Site
Delphinium tricorne dwarf larkspur white, blue, violet	Afternoon shade; likes lime
Dodecatheon meadia shooting-star white or light pink	Woodland; needs moisture and shade in the South
Echinacea purpurea purple coneflower magenta	Full sun
Elephantopus tomentosus elephant-foot pink, purple, rarely white	Woodland
Erigeron pulchellus robin's plantain lavender to white	Woodland or afternoon shade

Allegheny spurge makes a good replacement for Japanese spurge. Grow it for its mottled leaves. The blossom belongs to a plant of woodland phlox.

Erythrina herbacea
coral bean
red

Woodland
(zones 8 and 9)

Erythronium americanum
trout-lily
yellow, purple-backed petals

Woodland

Eupatorium coelestinum
mist flower
blue to reddish purple

Full sun or
afternoon shade

Eupatorium fistulosum
joe-pye weed
pink-purple

Full sun

Euphorbia corollata
(= E. pubentissima)
flowering spurge
white

Full sun

Gaillardia pulchella
Indian blanket, firewheel
yellow, gold, mahogany, some bicolors

Full sun

Gaultheria procumbens
wintergreen, teaberry
white flowers, scarlet fruit

Woodland; a
mountain plant

Geranium maculatum
cranesbill
lavender, purple, near white

Woodland or
afternoon shade

Gillenia trifoliata
Indian physic
white

Woodland or
afternoon shade

Gnaphalium obtusifolium
rabbit tobacco or sweet everlasting
white flowers, gray foliage

Full sun

Helenium autumnale
sneezeweed
yellow

Full sun

Helianthus species, including
   H. angustifolius, narrow-leaved sunflower
   H. hirsutus, rough sunflower
   H. mollis, ashy sunflower
   H. maximiliani, maximilian sunflower
All helianthus have yellow flowers.

Full sun

Heliopsis helianthoides
ox-eye
yellow

Full sun or
afternoon shade

Hepatica acutiloba and **H. americana**
liverleaf
bluish, pink, or white

Woodland

**Heterotheca graminifolia (= Chrysopsis
graminifolia)**
silk-grass
yellow

Full sun or
afternoon shade

Heterotheca mariana (= Chrysopsis mariana)
Maryland golden-aster
yellow

Full sun or
afternoon shade

Heuchera americana
alumroot
yellowish, delicate flowers

Afternoon shade;
sunny, dry sites

Heuchera villosa
alumroot
white

Woodland or
afternoon shade;
a mountain plant,
but adaptable if
given moist soil

Hexastylis arifolia
heart-leaf ginger, little brown jugs
brown, fleshy, hidden flowers

Woodland

Hibiscus coccineus
red swamp hibiscus
crimson to dark red

Full sun or
afternoon shade

Houstonia caerulea
bluet
blue, violet-purple, or white

Woodland or
afternoon shade

Hydrastis canadensis
goldenseal
white

Woodland

Hydrophyllum virginianum
waterleaf
lavender

Woodland

Hypericum species
St. Johnswort
yellow

Sun and
afternoon shade

Hypoxis hirsuta yellow star grass	Afternoon shade or full sun
Ipomopsis rubra standing cypress, Texas plume red, often spotted	Full sun; needs sandy soil
Iris cristata crested iris light violet-blue	Woodland or afternoon shade; moist soil
Iris verna dwarf iris violet-blue with orange stripe	Afternoon shade; drier sites
Iris hybrids of the Louisiana group violet-blue, yellow, red, brown, and bicolors	Full sun; marsh or water's-edge plants
Jeffersonia diphylla twinleaf white	Woodland; likes lime; a mountain plant, somewhat difficult elsewhere
Kosteletzkya virginica seashore mallow light pink, ephemeral flowers	Full sun

Liatris (gayfeather or blazing star)
species, including
  L. aspera; lavender
  L. graminifolia; lavender
  L. pycnostachya; rose-purple, white
  (dwarf cultivars available)
  L. squarrosa; lavender
  L. tenuifolia; lavender
	Full sun or
	afternoon shade;
	grass-leaved
	species prefer
	deep sand

Lilium, southern species, including
  L. catesbaei, pine lily (bogs); orange spotted
  L. michauxii, Carolina lily; reddish pink/yellow
  L. superbum, turk's-cap lily; reddish orange,
  heavily spotted
	Afternoon shade

Lobelia cardinalis cardinal-flower red, some with bronze foliage	Afternoon shade or woodland
Lobelia siphilitica great blue lobelia violet-blue	Afternoon shade or woodland

	Preferred Site
Lysimachia lanceolata var. *lanceolata* whorled loosestrife Do not confuse this yellow-flowered plant with *Lythrum salicaria,* purple loosestrife.	Full sun
Marshallia grandiflora Barbara's buttons light pink to rose	Afternoon shade or full sun; moist soil
Medeola virginiana Indian cucumber-root yellowish flowers, dark fruit	Woodland
Melanthium virginicum bunchflower creamy white	Woodland; wet soil
Mertensia virginica Virginia bluebells light violet-blue, pink buds	Woodland or afternoon shade
Mitchella repens partridgeberry white flowers, red berries	Woodland

Of the eighteen or so native trilliums, *Trillium luteum* is one of the easiest to grow beneath hardwoods. It prefers moist, fertile soils that are basic in reaction.

Monarda species, including
   M. citriodora, lemon mint; white to pink
   M. didyma, bee balm; many colors in cultivars
   M. fistulosa, wild bergamot; lavender to white
   M. punctata, dotted horsemint; yellowish,
   spotted purple
	Full sun or
	afternoon shade

Oenothera fruticosa sundrops waxy yellow	Full sun
Oenothera speciosa showy evening primrose pink	Full sun; invasive

Orchids of several woodland species, including
   Aplectrum hyemale, putty-root; yellowish brown
   Goodyera pubescens, rattlesnake-plantain; white
   Tipularia discolor, cranefly orchid; greenish
   yellow to bronze-purple
	Woodland

Orchids of several sun-loving species
(most of them moist-pineland plants),
including
   Habenaria ciliaris, yellow fringed orchid;
   yellow to orange
   H. nivea, snowy orchid; white
   Spiranthes species, ladies'-tresses; white
	Full sun or
	afternoon shade

Panax trifolius dwarf ginseng white, tinged pink	Woodland; a medicinal plant, not showy, slow to grow
Parthenium integrifolium American feverfew, wild quinine white	Full sun or afternoon shade

Penstemon species, including
   P. cobaea, foxglove penstemon; white
   to pale violet, spectacular
   P. digitalis, white penstemon
   P. smallii, Small's beard-tongue; lavender-pink
	Full sun or
	afternoon shade

Phacelia purshii fringed phacelia pale blue/white	Afternoon shade or full sun; delicate; plant in groups away from larger flowers

Phlox species, including
  P. carolina, thick-leaved phlox; numerous colors   Afternoon shade
  in cultivars   or full sun
  P. divaricata, woodland phlox, Louisiana phlox,   Woodland or
  or wild sweet William; pale violet-blue   afternoon shade
  P. pilosa, Ozark phlox, downy phlox; purple,   Woodland or
  pink, white   afternoon shade
  P. stolonifera, creeping phlox; several colors   Full sun or
  in cultivars   afternoon shade
  P. subulata, moss pink; many unusual, vivid   Full sun or afternoon
  shades in cultivars (very popular)   shade; dry sites

Podophyllum peltatum   Woodland;
may-apple   invasive
yellowish white, occasionally reddish

Polygonatum species   Woodland
Solomon's-seal
white or yellowish green

Polygonella americana   Full sun; deep
fringed polygonella   sandy soil
white, long-blooming

Pycnanthemum incanum   Afternoon shade
white horsemint   or full sun
silver-tipped foliage, white flowers; and
P. tenuifolium
common horsemint
white to pink, dotted purple

Pyrola rotundifolia var. *americana*   Woodland
shinleaf
white

Ratibida pinnata   Full sun
gray-head coneflower
yellow ray flowers, occasionally with dark bases

Rosa carolina   Full sun
Carolina wild rose
rose-pink

Rudbeckia species, including   Full sun
  R. hirta, black-eyed Susan
  R. triloba, thin-leaved coneflower
  R. fulgida var. *fulgida,* orange coneflower
All are yellow; some cultivars are orange
or have brown markings.

One of the best spots for merrybells, or bellwort, is on a steep, moist slope under hardwoods, where you can look up at the pendent bells.

	Preferred Site
Ruellia caroliniensis wild petunia lilac to lavender-blue	Afternoon shade or woodland
Salvia coccinea scarlet sage bright red; and ***S.lyrata*** lyre-leaved sage purple	Full sun
Sanguinaria canadensis bloodroot white, occasionally flushed pink	Woodland
Scutellaria integrifolia narrow-leaved scullcap blue or whitish	Full sun
Sedum ternatum stonecrop white	Woodland or afternoon sun; grow among rocks
Shortia galacifolia shortia, Oconee bells white	Woodland; moist soil; a mountain plant
Silene polypetala fringed catchfly pink An endangered species; buy only plants propagated under a permit.	Woodland
Silene virginica fire pink dark red	Woodland or afternoon shade
Silphium dentatum no common name yellow; var. ***gatesii*** has short plants	Full sun
Sisyrinchium atlanticum blue-eyed grass light blue	Woodland or afternoon shade
Smilacina racemosa false Solomon's-seal greenish white	Woodland

Smilax herbacea
smilax
greenish flowers; grown for foliage
Woodland

Solidago species, including
  S. caesia, blue-stemmed goldenrod
  S. curtisii
  S. odora, sweet goldenrod
  S. sphacelata, false goldenrod
  S. stricta, slim goldenrod
All goldenrods have yellow or golden yellow flowers.

Woodland or
afternoon shade

Full sun

Spigelia marilandica
Indian pink
red/yellow
Full sun or
afternoon shade

Stokesia laevis
Stokes' aster
violet-blue, occasionally white; pink or purple
cultivars available
Full sun or
afternoon shade

Tiarella cordifolia
foamflower
white to pinkish white
Woodland

Tradescantia species, including
  T. hirsuticaulis, hairy-stemmed spiderwort
  T. subaspera, zigzag spiderwort
  T. virginiana, common spiderwort
All come in violet-blue, purple, and white.

Full sun or
afternoon shade

Invasive

Trillium species, including
  T. catesbaei, rosy wakerobin; pink or white
  T. cuneatum, whippoorwill-flower; purple to
  burgundy
  T. grandiflorum, large-flowered trillium; white,
  aging to rose
  T. luteum, lemon-scented trillium; yellow
  T. undulatum, painted trillium; white with red chevrons
  T. vaseyi, Vasey's trillium (large plants);
  maroon, occasionally white
Woodland

Uvularia species
bellwort, merrybells
yellow
Woodland

Verbena canadensis
rose vervain
reddish purple in the wild; many colors available
in cultivars
Full sun or
afternoon shade

	Preferred Site
Vernonia noveboracensis and other ***Vernonia*** species ironweed reddish purple	Full sun or afternoon shade
Veronicastrum virginicum Culver's root white	Full sun; likes lime and moisture

Viola species, including
  V. floridana, Florida violet; purple
  V. hastata, halberd violet; yellow with silver stripes
  V. pedata, birdfoot violet; blue, white, pink, and bicolors
  V. priceana, Confederate violet; blue, violet, or white with contrasting eye
  V. sororia, woolly blue violet; dark blue, purple, violet, gray, white
  V. walteri, Walter's violet; bluish violet
	Woodland or afternoon shade
	
	Invasive

Zephranthes treatiae and ***Z. atamasco*** both called atamasco or rain lily white, occasionally pink or rose	Woodland or afternoon shade

 ## GRASSES AND SEDGES

	Preferred Site
Carex species evergreen sedges	Woodland or full-sun marsh plants, but adaptable
Chasmanthium latifolium river oats	Full sun; water's edge
Cymophyllus fraseri Fraser's sedge rare, white-flowered woodland species	Woodland
Deschampsia spp. tufted hairgrass	Full sun or afternoon shade
Erianthus giganteus sugarcane plume grass	Full sun
Juncus coriaceus and ***J. effusus*** rush	Full sun; marsh plants

FERNS

All ferns grow best in woodland sites.

Adiantum pedatum
American maidenhair fern

Asplenium platyneuron
ebony spleenwort

Athyrium filix-femina var.
asplenioides
southern lady fern

Dryopteris ludoviciana
Louisiana shield fern
evergreen in the Deep South

Dryopteris marginalis
marginal shield fern
evergreen

Osmunda species, including
  O. cinnamomea,
  cinnamon fern
  O. claytoniana,
  interrupted fern;
  native to the North
  O. regalis, royal fern   Wetlands

Polystichum acrostichoides   Adaptable
Christmas fern
evergreen

Thelypteris kunthii   Likes lime
southern shield fern

Thelypteris noveboracensis   Can be
New York fern   invasive

Woodwardia areolata   Likes wet
netted chain fern   soil

It is hard to believe that this beautiful and well-mannered spring-blooming woodland plant, *Stellaria pubera* (giant chickweed), is related to the pestiferous chickweed of lawns and gardens.

Prairie Wildflowers and Grasses

THE STAFF of the Chicago Botanic Garden supplied this list, which includes prairie flowers and grasses that grow well for them at Glencoe, Illinois. The principal flower color(s) of the wild species appears beneath the common name.

SPRING-FLOWERING SPECIES

	Notes
Anemone patens (= Pulsatilla patens) pasqueflower blue-violet; naturalized	Small plants; grow in groups away from large plants
Baptisia leucophaea prairie false indigo white or creamy	Takes four years to flower after seed is planted
Camassia scilloides eastern camas blue, violet-blue, white	Mass for best effect; plant bulbs 3 to 5 inches deep in fall
Dodecatheon meadia shooting-star magenta, lavender, white	Easy to establish
Geum triflorum prairie smoke purplish	Small; plant in groups away from large grass or flower species
Heuchera richardsonii alumroot small greenish flowers in open sprays	Slow to develop
Ranunculus rhomboides prairie buttercup yellow	Likes dry soil; plant away from larger species
Zizia aptera heart-leaved golden alexanders; and **Z. aurea** golden alexanders both yellow	Self-sows easily

Allium cernuum
nodding onion
rose or white

Self-sows easily; also
increases vegetatively

Amorpha canescens
lead plant
violet-purple

Slow to establish

Anemone cylindrica
thimbleweed
greenish white

Likes small companions

Asclepias incarnata
swamp milkweed
pink, occasionally white

Rodents eat the crowns, rabbits
eat the foliage — protect plants;
monarch butterfly host plant

Asclepias sullivantii
prairie milkweed
purplish rose

Slow-growing the first year;
butterfly host plant

Asclepias tuberosa
butterfly weed
orange, yellow, orange-red,
other colors in cultivars

Easy to grow from seeds, but
slow; difficult to transplant;
butterfly host plant

Aster ptarmicoides
white upland aster
white disk and ray flowers

Forms persistent clumps

Baptisia leucantha
white false indigo
clear white

Treat seeds with inoculant

Coreopsis palmata
stiff tickseed
yellow

Spreads vegetatively

Desmodium canadense
tick trefoil, beggar's-lice
purple

Quick to establish from
inoculated seeds

Echinacea pallida
pale-purple coneflower
light rose, magenta, occasionally white

Likes dry sites

Echinacea purpurea
purple prairie coneflower
magenta

More vigorous than **E. pallida**;
establishes quickly

	Notes
Eryngium yuccifolium rattlesnake-master silvery white	Quick to establish; self-sows
Euphorbia corollata flowering spurge, tramp's spurge white	Slow to establish
Heliopsis helianthoides false sunflower, ox-eye pale yellow, several cultivars	Establishes and spreads quickly
Liatris aspera blazing star, gayfeather rose-purple	Rodents like the corms

From Minnesota to Texas, concerned citizens are involved in restoring or constructing prairies. This Texas researcher, Barbara Anthony, develops reliable methods of propagating southern prairie species and cooperates in restoration projects. The row of *Liatris* was planted to produce seeds.

Liatris pycnostachya blazing star, gayfeather rose-purple	Seed germinates over a long period; grows tall
Monarda fistulosa wild bergamot lavender, lilac, rose	Self-sows easily; spreads quickly from roots; susceptible to mildew unless thinned
Oenothera pilosella sundrops yellow	Establishes quickly; spreads vegetatively
Parthenium integrifolium American feverfew, wild quinine white	Long-flowering; very attractive but little-known
Penstemon digitalis tall white penstemon clear white	Self-sows easily; needs support of surrounding plants to keep it from breaking at the base because of flower weight
Petalostemon candidum white prairie clover white; and *P. purpureum (= Dalea purpurea)* purple prairie clover violet to crimson	Scarify and inoculate seeds; germinate in dryish sand; rabbits like foliage
Phlox glaberrima smooth phlox purple to pink, occasionally white	Seeds germinate sporadically; mice eat crowns, rabbits like foliage; benefits from supporting grass
Physostegia virginiana obedient plant rose-purple; several cultivars available	Grows moderately quickly; spreads from roots; benefits from grass support
Potentilla arguta tall cinquefoil creamy white	Establishes quickly; self-sows
Ratibida pinnata prairie coneflower yellow ray flowers	Establishes quickly; self-sows easily
Rosa carolina pasture rose rose-pink	Easy to grow; spreads from rhizomes
Rudbeckia hirta black-eyed Susan yellow ray flowers	A short-lived, self-sowing perennial

Rudbeckia subtomentosa
sweet coneflower
yellow ray flowers, brown-purple disks

Establishes quickly from seeds

Ruellia humilis
wild petunia
lavender to bluish

Easy to establish

Silphium integrifolium
rosinweed
yellow

Easy if transplanted quickly; develops long taproot; blooms second year from seeds

Silphium laciniatum
compass plant
yellow; deeply cut leaves

Same as **S. integrifolium,** except blooms third year or later from seeds

Silphium terebinthinaceum
prairie dock
yellow; very broad leaves

Same as **S. laciniatum**

Tradescantia ohiensis
spiderwort
blue, purple, rose, occasionally white

Quick to establish; self-sows

Veronicastrum virginicum
Culver's root
white spires

Plants stay small the first year

🙢 AUTUMN-FLOWERING SPECIES

Aster azureus
sky-blue aster
deep blue to violet

Self-sows easily

Aster laevis
smooth aster
blue to pale purple

Self-sows easily

Aster novae-anglia
New England aster
deep violet-purple with yellow centers; several colors in cultivars

Self-sows easily

Aster oblongifolius
aromatic aster
violet-blue, occasionally rose-pink

Self-sows easily; spreads quickly vegetatively

Aster sericeus
silky aster
deep violet to rose-purple

Likes drier sites

Gentiana andrewsii
bottle gentian
blue, ages to purple

Plant in groups for mass effect

Solidago speciosa
showy goldenrod
golden yellow

Showy but not weedy; self-sows

 SHORTER GRASSES

Bouteloua curtipendula side-oats grama	Good for mixing with the smaller, weaker flowers
Bromus kalmii prairie brome	A cool-season grass
Buchloe dactyloides buffalo grass[1]	A warm-season, carpet-forming, drought-resistant grass
Koeleria cristata June grass	A cool-season grass
Schizachryium scoparium little bluestem shorter than big bluestem but still relatively tall	Good support grass for floppy flowers; likes dry sites
Sporobolus heterolepsis northern dropseed	

 TALLER GRASSES

Panicum virgatum switchgrass	Good support for floppy flowers; cultivars with reddish foliage are available as plants
Sorghastrum nutans Indiangrass	A nice ornamental

---

[1] I added buffalo grass to the list. Although it forms a fairly thick carpet, it doesn't assert itself until warm weather, when the perennial flowers have already made a good start.

LANDSCAPE architect and prairie specialist Guy Sternberg supplied the following list of prairie wildflowers and native grasses that grow well in central Illinois. Note the differences between his list and the one supplied by the Chicago Botanic Garden. Mr. Sternberg leans toward the shorter, more easily managed, and more colorful native species.

Please note that Mr. Sternberg uses special care when planting prairie species of **Helianthus** (sunflower) and **Solidago** (goldenrod), as they inhibit the growth of other species around them. He advises minimizing the problem by planting sunflowers and goldenrods in masses instead of scattering them. Also, in his area, **Rudbeckia** species (black-eyed Susan) tend to self-sow aggressively and may push out slower-growing prairie wildflowers.

 SMALL WILDFLOWERS (under 2 feet tall)

	Notes
Antennaria neglecta pussytoes white	Early-blooming ground cover
Asclepias tuberosa butterfly weed orange, yellow, red-orange	Brilliant; occasionally grows taller. Direct-seed into new prairies
Cassia fasciculata partridge-pea yellow	Reseeding annual; a good nurse plant
Heterotheca camporum **(= Chrysopsis camporum)** golden aster yellow	Low plant for massing
Lithospermum canescens puccoon orange-yellow	Start from root cuttings
Phlox bifida phlox lavender, lilac, white	Early color, shade-tolerant; downy cultivars available

MEDIUM-TALL WILDFLOWERS (2 to 5 feet)

Asclepias incarnata
red milkweed
rose, occasionally white

Actually rose-pink; few prairie plants bloom pure red

Aster ericoides
heath aster
white, occasionally blue or pink

Shade-tolerant

Aster oblongifolius
aromatic aster
blue; a pink cultivar is available

The most useful blue aster; avoid its aggressive relatives

Baptisia leucantha
wild white indigo
white

A legume; brilliant flowers

Cassia marilandica
senna
yellow

A tall legume

Ceanothus americanus
New Jersey tea
white

Woody basal stems

Coreopsis lanceolata
prairie coreopsis
yellow

Selected cultivars are available

Echinacea pallida
pale purple coneflower
rose, magenta, rarely white

Strongly weeping petals

Echinacea paradoxa
golden coneflower

Similar to **E. pallida,** but with yellow flowers

Echinacea purpurea
purple coneflower

White, pink, and rose cultivars available in addition to the wild purple species

Eryngium yuccifolium
rattlesnake-master
grayish white

Bristly flowers; good winter foliage

Liatris species
blazing stars
pink to purple

White cultivars available

Monarda didyma
White, pink, lavender, and red
bee balm

cultivars are available, but some are susceptible to mildew

	Notes
Monarda fistulosa wild bergamot lavender, lilac, rose	Resistant to mildew if thinned
Penstemon cobaea purple beard-tongue	A colorful early bloomer
Penstemon digitalis white beard-tongue clear white	Shade-tolerant
Petalostemon purpureum *(= Dalea purpurea)* purple prairie clover	Buds are covered with silvery hairs; petals open from the base up on the cloverlike "heads"
Physostegia virginiana false dragonhead	White, pink, rose, and red cultivars available
Ratibida pinnata gray-head coneflower	Can grow taller than the *Echinacea* genus
Vernonia fasciculata ironweed rose-purple	Grows taller in good soil

TALL WILDFLOWERS (more than 5 feet)

Silphium laciniatum compass plant yellow	Attractive winter foliage; flower stalks may lean
Silphium perfoliatum cup plant yellow	Interesting square stems; leaves hold dew for wildlife
Silphium terebinthinaceum prairie dock yellow	Large leaves; needs room; flower stalks may lean

TALL GRASSES (5 feet and taller)

Andropogon gerardi big bluestem	Can become aggressive; may lean; good winter color
Erianthus alopecuroides plume grass	Shade-tolerant

Sorghastrum nutans Indian grass	Slightly shorter, similar to ***Erianthus alopecuroides***
Tripsacum dactyloides gama grass	Large, coarse-featured, attractive plumes; a distant relative of maize

🎶 MEDIUM-TALL GRASSES (under 5 feet)

Bouteloua curtipendula side-oats grama	Interesting seedheads
Chasmanthium latifolium inland sea oats, river oats	Attractive seedheads in winter, shade-tolerant
Elymus canadensis nodding wild rye	Spreading but not aggressive; shade-tolerant; cool-season grass
Schizachyrium scoparium little bluestem	Superior winter color

Each of the various perennial sunflower species has developed local ecotypes. This one, grown by Barbara Anthony, is comparatively low-growing and is tidier and less likely to blow over than some of its extremely tall relatives.

DR. MAY WRIGHT, educational chairman of the Minnesota Native Plant Society, supplied this list of relatively easy-to-grow wildflower species native to Minnesota.

 FOR FULL SUN

Anemone patens American pasqueflower	**Lupinus perennis** lupine
Asclepias tuberosa butterfly weed	**Monarda fistulosa** wild bergamot
Asclepias verticillata whorled milkweed	**Petalostemon purpureum** prairie smoke
Aster novae-anglia New England aster	**Phlox pilosa** prairie phlox
Cassia fasciculata partridge-pea, prairie senna	**Ranunculus fascicularis** early buttercup
Dodecatheon meadia shooting-star	**Rudbeckia hirta** black-eyed Susan
Liatris aspera rough blazing star	

 FOR SHADE

Aquilegia canadensis wild columbine	**Lobelia siphilitica** blue lobelia
Asarum canadense wild ginger	**Mitella diphylla** bishop's cap
Geranium maculatum wild geranium	**Phlox divaricata** blue phlox
Hepatica americana round-leaved hepatica	**Sanguinaria canadensis** bloodroot
Isopyrum biternatum false rue-anemone	**Uvularia grandiflora** large-flowered bellwort
Lobelia cardinalis cardinal-flower	**Viola canadensis** Canada violet

Starflower is native to moist woodlands in north central and northeastern states. Though its individual flowers are small, they are so numerous that they make quite a show in spring.

Dr. Wright commented, "Some of the shade-tolerant species might adapt to sunny situations if watered with drip irrigation. If you don't have trees in your yard, plant these species where they will get afternoon shade from walls or buildings."

I asked whether members of the Minnesota Native Plant Society usually direct-seed wildflowers or start with plants. She said, "Our members report that direct seeding is cheaper and works satisfactorily for the easier species, such as wild bergamot, partridge-pea, and black-eyed Susan. We usually transplant some of the small or slow-growing species — American pasqueflower, shooting-star, bottle gentian, and fringed gentian, to name a few. Often we use both methods, direct-seeding the easy species to get quick color and erosion control, and plugging in transplants of the more difficult species."

Certain non-native meadow or marsh flowers can escape and become troublesome weeds. Dr. Wright recommends that these not be planted in Minnesota: **Chicorium intybus,** chicory; **Chrysanthemum leucanthemum,** ox-eye daisy; **Daucus carota,** Queen Anne's lace; **Euphorbia esula,** leafy spurge; **Hieracium aurantiacum,** orange hawkweed; and **Lythrum salicaria,** purple loosestrife.

High-Altitude Western Wildflowers

ROBERT HEAPES provided this list of wildflowers that do well in his Parker, Colorado, garden. He has had excellent success with plants from very diverse climates and soils. Some of these species might grow in your area.

EASY TO GROW

	Propagation Method		Propagation Method
Anemone multifida windflower	Seed	*Callirhoe involucrata* purple poppy-mallow	Seed
Antennaria parvifolia pussytoes	Division	*Campanula rotundifolia* harebell	Seed
Aquilegia caerulea blue columbine	Seed	*Clarkia pulchella* ragged robin	Seed
Aquilegia saximontana dwarf columbine	Seed	*Lewisia cotyledon* bitterroot	Seed

Thermopsis divaricarpa golden banner	Division	***Viola pedata*** birdfoot violet	Seed
Verbena canadensis verbena	Cuttings		

✎ SLIGHTLY MORE DIFFICULT TO GROW

Erigeron compositus cutleaf daisy	Seed	***Lewisia columbiana*** bitterroot	Seed
Heterotheca villosa golden-aster	Seed	***Papaver alpinum*** alpine poppy	Seed

Lilium philadelphicum (wood lily) is becoming rare in the wild.
It prefers sandy soil in open woods or fields.

	Propagation Method		Propagation Method
Penstemon caespitosus mat penstemon	Cuttings	*Townsendia parryi* Parry's Easter daisy	Seed
Polemonium caeruleum Jacob's ladder	Seed	*Townsendia rothrockii* Rothrock's Easter daisy	Seed
Potentilla nevadensis prostrate cinquefoil	Cuttings	*Zauschneria californica*[1] red zauschneria	Cuttings
Sisyrinchium macrocarpum yellow-eyed grass	Seed	*Zauschneria garrettii*[1] orange zauschneria	Cuttings
Sisyrinchium montana blue-eyed grass	Seed		

[1]Some authorities list the *Zauschneria* species under the genus *Epilobium*.

MODERATELY DIFFICULT TO GROW

Erigeron simplex one-headed daisy	Seed	*Penstemon teucriodes* germander penstemon	Cuttings
Iris missouriensis blue flag	Seed	*Phlox idahoensis* Idaho phlox	Cuttings
Penstemon cardwellii cascade penstemon	Cuttings	*Phlox nana* Santa Fe phlox	Cuttings
Penstemon davidsonii Davidson's penstemon	Cuttings	*Phlox pulvinata* tundra phlox	Cuttings

DIFFICULT TO GROW

Besseya montana alpine kittentails	Seed	*Phlox hoodii* Wyoming phlox	Cuttings
Mahonia repens hollygrape	Cuttings	*Sine acaulis* moss campion	Cuttings
Phlox diffusa Mt. Hood phlox	Cuttings		

VERY DIFFICULT TO GROW

Arctotstaphylos uva-ursa kinnikinnik	Cuttings	*Phlox mesoleuca* Mexican phlox	Cuttings

GEYATA AJILVSGI, a Native American, wrote the book that got me started on wildflowers, *Wild Flowers of the Big Thicket.* Later I purchased her more comprehensive book, *Wildflowers of Texas.* She kindly supplied this list of native wildflowers that she feels will grow relatively quickly and easily from seeds or divisions. Actually, her list was longer, but I took the liberty of deleting a few species. John Thomas, of Wildseed, Incorporated, marked with an asterisk those species that can be readily purchased as Texas-grown seeds after the 1992 harvest. Great Plains wildflower seed producers grow some of the others, and Texas wildflower nurseries offer plants of some species.

 **WHITE FLOWERS**

	Annual, Biennial, or Perennial[1]	Preferred Site[2]
Argemone albiflora subsp. ***texana*** white prickly poppy	Annual or perennial	Full sun; sandy or gravelly soil
Claytonia virginica spring beauty or pink	Perennial	Full sun or light shade; sandy, fertile soil
Delphinium virescens prairie larkspur	Perennial	Full sun; moist soil; adaptable, but poisonous
Eriogonum annuum wild buckwheat	Annual	Full sun; dry, sandy or gravelly soil

[1]Annuals include both winter and summer annuals. Biennials form a rosette the first season and bloom the second; they occasionally act like an annual or a perennial. Plants listed as perennial are perennial in their native Texas habitat but may require winter protection or treatment as an annual in other areas, depending on their winter-hardiness and resistance to humid conditions.
[2]"Full sun" means at least six hours of sun daily. "Light shade" means dappled sunlight; plants should not be sited where they have competition from surface-rooted trees. "Moderate shade" means less than six hours of dappled sunlight. Plants that need lime grow in their native habitat in chalky soil, among calcium-bearing rocks, or in neutral or basic soil derived from limestone or other calcium-bearing rocks.

	Annual, Biennial, or Perennial	Preferred Site
Erythronium albidum white dogtooth violet	Perennial	Light to moderate shade; needs humus, likes lime
Euphorbia bicolor snow-on-the-prairie; and	Annual	Full sun; adaptable
E. marginata snow-on-the-mountain	Annual	Full sun; adaptable
Gaura lindheimeri white gaura	Perennial	Full sun; moist, fertile soil
Heliotropium convolvulaceum fragrant heliotrope	Annual	Full sun; sandy soil
Ipomopsis grandiflora pale trumpets	Annual or biennial	Full sun; rocky or gravelly soil

Here *Gaura lindheimerii* is used as a tall white accent plant in a bed of perennials.

Melampodium leucanthum Plains black-foot	Perennial	Full sun; likes lime
* *Monarda lindheimeri* Lindheimer bee balm	Perennial	Full sun; gravelly soil, needs lime
Oenothera engelmannii Englemann's evening primrose	Annual	Full sun; sandy soil
Petalostemon multiflorum *(= Dalea multiflora)* white prairie clover	Perennial	Full sun; dry, limey soil
Polygonatum biflorum great Solomon's-seal	Perennial	Light to moderate shade; moist soil; needs humus
Tephrosia onbrychoides multibloom tephrosia	Perennial	Full sun; sandy soil
Viola primulifolia primrose-leaved violet	Perennial	Light to moderate shade; moist, slightly acid soil
Zinnia acerosa dwarf zinnia	Perennial	Full sun; likes lime

 ## YELLOW OR GOLDEN FLOWERS

Aletris aurea colic root	Perennial	Full sun; moist, acid soil
* *Baileya multiradiata* desert marigold	Annual or perennial	Full sun; sandy or rocky soil
Calylophus drummondianus square-bud day primrose	Annual or perennial	Full sun; sandy or rocky soil
* *Cassia fasciculata* partridge-pea	Annual	Full sun; sandy, acid soil
Castilleja purpurea lemon paintbrush	Perennial	Full sun; sandy or rocky soil; semiparasitic on grass and other wildflowers
* *Coreopsis basalis* coreopsis	Perennial	Full sun; sandy soil; the variety **wrightii** needs lime
* *Coreopsis tinctoria* calliopsis or plains coreopsis	Annual	Full sun; adaptable; prefers moist soil

	Annual, Biennial, or Perennial	Preferred Site
* *Dracopis amplexicaulis* clasping-leaved coneflower	Annual	Full sun; moist, heavy soil
Dyssodia tenuiloba bristle-leaf dyssodia	Annual or perennial	Full sun; sandy or loamy soil
Eschscholzia mexicana Mexican gold poppy	Annual	Full sun; rocky or gravelly soil
Gaillardia suavis fragrant gaillardia	Annual	Full sun; sandy or loamy soil
Helianthus angustifolius swamp sunflower	Perennial	Full sun; moist, fertile soil
Linum rigidum var. *berlandieri* stiff-stem flax	Annual	Full sun; sandy, gravelly soil; needs lime
Monarda punctata spotted bee balm	Perennial	Full sun; sandy or rocky soil
* *Oenothera missouriensis* (= *O. macrocarpa*) Missouri primrose	Perennial	Full sun; dry, rocky soil; needs lime
* *Ratibida columnaris* Mexican hat	Perennial	Full sun; adaptable; needs lime
* *Rudbeckia angustifolia* var. *hirta* brown-eyed or black-eyed Susan	Annual or perennial	Full sun; adaptable
Solidago petiolaris downy goldenrod	Perennial	Full sun; sandy or gravelly soil
Sphaeralcea angustifolia copper mallow	Perennial	Full sun; sandy or rocky soil; needs lime
Thelesperma filifolium green thread	Annual	Full sun; dry soil; needs lime
Wedelia hispida (= *Zeximenia hispida*) wedelia	Perennial	Full sun; dry, gravelly soil, needs hairy lime
Zinnia grandiflora zinnia	Perennial	Full sun; dry soil; Plains needs lime

RED, REDDISH ORANGE, OR PINK FLOWERS

Argemone sanguinea rose prickly poppy	Annual, biennial, or perennial	Full sun; adaptable
* ***Asclepias tuberosa*** butterfly weed	Perennial	Full sun; adaptable
Callirhoe involucrata winecup	Perennial	Full sun; sandy, gravelly soil
* ***Castilleja indivisa*** Indian or Texas paintbrush	Annual or biennial	Full sun; moist, sandy loam; semi-parasitic on grass
Echinacea sanguinea purple coneflower	Perennial	Full sun to light shade; sandy, gravelly soil
* ***Gaillardia amblyodon*** red gaillardia	Annual	Full sun; deep sand
* ***Gaillardia pulchella*** Indian blanket	Annual	Full sun; adaptable
Gaura coccinea scarlet gaura	Perennial	Full sun; sandy soil
Hibiscus cardiophyllus tulipan del monte	Perennial	Full sun; dry soil; needs lime
Indigofera miniata scarlet pea	Perennial	Full sun; sandy soil
* ***Ipomopsis rubra*** standing cypress or Texas plume	Biennial	Full sun or light shade; dry, gravelly soil; needs lime
* ***Lobelia cardinalis*** cardinal-flower	Perennial	Light to moderate shade; moist, rich soil
* ***Oenothera speciosa*** showy primrose	Perennial	Full sun; adaptable
Penstemon harvardii Harvard penstemon	Perennial	Full sun; rocky, gravelly soil; needs lime
* ***Phlox drummondii*** subsp. ***wilcoxiana*** Drummond or annual phlox	Annual	Full sun; deep, sandy soil
Phlox pilosa downy or prairie phlox	Perennial	Full sun; adaptable

	Annual, Biennial, or Perennial	Preferred Site
Rhexia mariana Maryland meadow beauty	Perennial	Full sun; wet or moist, fertile soil
* *Salvia coccinea* tropical sage	Perennial	Full sun; adaptable
Stachys drummondii pink mint	Annual or biennial	Full sun; adaptable
Verbena bipinnatifida Dakota vervain	Perennial	Full sun; dry, sandy soil; needs lime
Verbena canadensis rose vervain	Perennial	Full sun to light shade; sandy or rocky soil

❦ BLUE, LAVENDER, VIOLET, OR PURPLE FLOWERS

Amsonia illustris showy blue star	Perennial	Full sun to light shade; moist or wet soil
Baptisia australis wild blue indigo	Perennial	Full sun; clay soil
Centrosema virginianum butterfly pea	Perennial	Full sun to light shade; sandy soil
Dalea lasiathera purple dalea	Perennial	Full sun; poor, dry soil; needs lime
Delphinium carolinianum Carolina delphinium	Perennial	Full sun; dry, sandy soil
Eryngium leavenworthii eryngo	Annual	Full sun; heavy soil; needs lime
Eupatorium coelestinum mist flower	Perennial	Full sun; moist or wet soil
* *Eustoma grandiflorum* Texas bluebells	Perennial	Full sun; moist soil; adaptable
Gilia rigidula blue gilia	Perennial	Full sun; dry, sandy or rocky soil; needs lime
Iris virginica southern iris	Perennial	Full sun; rich, moist or wet soil

The long-stemmed *Marshallia tenuifolia* (Barbara's buttons) is native from
northern Florida and southern Georgia through east Texas. It grows best
on pineland savannas but is often seen on open land where the soil is
moist. Certain other *Marshallia* species are rare.

* *Liatris mucronata* narrow-leaved gayfeather	Perennial	Full sun; adaptable; needs lime
* *Liatris squarrosa* blazing star	Perennial	Full sun; adaptable; needs lime
* *Lupinus subcarnosus* sandyland bluebonnet (often lumped with Texas bluebonnets)	Annual	Full sun; deep, sandy or rocky, poor soil
* *Lupinus texensis* Texas bluebonnet	Annual	Same as **L. subcarnosus**
* *Machaeranthera* *tanacetifolia* tahoka daisy or tansy aster	Annual	Full sun; sandy soil

	Annual, Biennial, or Perennial	Preferred Site
* *Monarda citriodora* lemon mint	Perennial	Full sun to light shade; adaptable
Monarda fistulosa wild bergamot	Perennial	Full sun to light shade; adaptable
* *Nemophila phacelioides* baby-blue-eyes	Annual	Full sun to light shade; moist soil; adaptable
Oxalis violacea violet wood sorrel	Perennial	Light to moderate shade; dry, sandy or rocky soil

The beautiful Texas native *Eustoma grandiflorum* (Texas bluebells or prairie gentian) grows on heavy soil in moist sites. It has been hybridized for garden use; its seeds are sold as lisianthus.

* *Petalostemon purpureum* (= *Dalea purpurea*) purple prairie clover	Perennial	Full sun; sandy soil
Phacelia patuliflora purple phacelia	Annual	Full sun; sandy soil
Physostegia pulchella beautiful false dragonhead	Annual	Full sun to light shade; moist to wet soil, adaptable
Ruellia nudiflora violet ruellia	Perennial	Full sun to light shade; adaptable
* *Salvia azurea,* var. *grandiflora* blue sage	Perennial	Full sun to light shade; dry, sandy or rocky soil
Salvia farinacea mealycup, blue salvia	Perennial	Full sun to light shade; dry, sandy or rocky soil
Scutellaria drummondii skullcap	Annual or perennial	Full sun; adaptable
* *Sisyrinchium pruinosum* dotted blue-eyed grass	Perennial	Full sun to light shade; adaptable
Tradescantia occidentalis prairie spiderwort	Perennial	Full sun to light shade; adaptable
Tradescantia ohiensis Ohio spiderwort	Perennial	Full sun to light shade; adaptable
Vernonia baldwinii western ironweed	Perennial	Full sun to light shade; rich, loamy soil
Viola pedata birdfoot violet	Perennial	Full sun; dry, poor, rocky or sandy soil

Note: Seeds of some of these species may be difficult to find. However, Texan and southwestern seed companies are expanding their lists of native herbaceous species and are beginning to sell these species to seedsmen and wildflower enthusiasts in other states. In my opinion, Texas wildflowers offer exciting possibilities for other parts of the country, especially the mid-South and Southeast. However, most species that grow as perennials in Texas must be treated as annuals in zone 6 and farther north. Although the Texas annuals reseed in their native habitats, they are not likely to repeat in eastern gardens north of zone 7. Also, some of the leguminous species, such as the bluebonnets, are difficult to start from seeds without special treatment, and difficult to grow unless the seeds are inoculated with the nitrogen-fixing bacteria that are present in Texan soils. Texan prairies have intense sun, high heat, long growing seasons, and neutral to alkaline soils — conditions that are difficult to reproduce in other parts of the United States — but east Texan fields and woodlands provide much the same habitats as the Southeast.

JUDITH PHILLIPS of Bernardo Beach Plant Farm, in Veguita, New Mexico, supplied this list of wildflowers from her state with potential for garden use. The usual flower color of the wild species is listed beneath its common name.

	New Mexico Habitat	**Preferred Moisture**
Allium cernuum nodding onion rose to white	Northern, higher elevations	Moderate to moist
Antennaria rosea pussytoes white	Mountains	Dry
Argemone ssp. prickly poppy white, yellow, red	Plains	Dry
Berlandiera lyrata chocolate flower yellow ray flowers, maroon disks	Plains, especially central	Low to moderate
Gaillardia aristata blanketflower yellow ray flowers, purple or yellow disks	Plains	Low to moderate
Liatris punctata spotted gayfeather pinkish purple	Plains, especially east	Low to moderate
Linum lewisii blue flax light blue	Higher elevations	Moderate
Melampodium leucanthum blackfoot daisy white ray flowers, yellow disks	Plains	Low to moderate
Oenothera caespitosa white-tufted evening primrose large white, fading to pink	Plains and mesas	Low

Oenothera speciosa Mexican evening primrose pink	Southern foothills	Low to moderate
Penstemon ambiguus bush penstemon white with deep rose throat	Plains and washes	Low
Penstemon barbatus scarlet bugler red, occasionally pink	Foothills	Low to moderate
Penstemon cardinalis cardinal penstemon red	Higher elevations	Low to moderate
Penstemon pinifolius pineleaf penstemon red	Dry slopes, south-west	Low
Penstemon pseudospectabilis desert penstemon rose-purple	Dry slopes, south-west	Low
Penstemon strictus Rocky Mountain penstemon dark blue	Higher elevations	Low to moderate

So many hybrids and selections have been made from *Rudbeckia hirta*, the rugged native black-eyed Susan, that the unimproved wild species is hard to find. Black-eyed Susan is an eastern and prairie flower, but related coneflowers are scattered from coast to coast.

	New Mexico Habitat	Preferred Moisture
Petalostemon purpureum **(= Dalea purpurea)** purple prairie clover intense pink florets, darker disks	Plains, north and central	Low to moderate
Ratibida columnaris Mexican hat or coneflower yellow or mahogany ray flowers	Plains and foot-hills	Moderate
Salvia azurea subsp. **grandiflora** blue or pitcher sage gentian blue	Plains and foot-hills, north and central	Moderate
Salvia greggii autumn or cherry sage many colors available in cultivars	5000–7000 ft. elevations	Well-drained soil; adaptable
Sphaeralcea coccinea scarlet globemallow orange-pink to orange-red	Plains and mesas	Low; a bit difficult
Verbena bipinnatifida fern verbena lavender-purple	Open pine forests and sandy roadsides	Sandy to gravelly, well-drained soil
Vernonia baldwinii ironweed reddish purple	Eastern plains	Moderate to moist
Zinnia grandiflora desert zinnia yellow ray flowers, orange centers	Grows everywhere in New Mexico	Dry

----

Note: From observing how wildflower enthusiasts grow western and southwestern pentstemons and other low-moisture species in the East and Southeast, I have come to the conclusion that excellent drainage combined with adequate moisture retention is the secret. One of the best ways to amend soil to simulate dry habitats is to add 10 to 15 percent granite meal by volume (more with clay soil, less with sand), plus 5 percent sphagnum peat moss, building up the beds to stand three to four inches higher than the surrounding soil. The sharp-edged particles of granite meal will keep the soil open and well drained during the winter, when soggy soil can reduce survival rates, and during summer storms, when wet soil can suffocate roots. Graded, bean-sized granite gravel is even better, but it is difficult to get except directly from a quarry.

Native Californian Plants for Garden Use

THIS LIST of relatively easy-to-grow, decorative, and adaptable herbaceous plants and companion shrubs native to California was compiled by George Waters, a long-time friend and the editor of *Pacific Horticulture* magazine. He stressed that most native Californian plants are best grown on ground that drains quickly — a hillside site can't be bettered. He added, "Success in cultivation will depend on local soil, climate, and the diligence of the gardener."

 ## ANNUALS

	Principal Color
Clarkia concinna red ribbons	Pink
Collinsia grandiflora blue lips	Blue bicolor with dark lower lip
Collinsia heterophylla purple Chinese houses	Violet or purple bicolor
Coreopsis douglasii coreopsis	Yellow
Eschscholzia californica California poppy ("the essential California wildflower")	Gold, yellow; many colors available in cultivars
Gilia aurea (= Linanthus aureus) ***golden gilia***	Yellow, often spotted
Gilia dichotoma ***(= Linanthus dichotomus)*** evening snow	White with contrasting throat
Layia glandulosa White layia	White; subspecies ***lutea*** is yellow
Layia platyglossa tidy-tips	Yellow with creamy white tips
Lupinus densiflorus white whorl lupine	White, yellow, rose, purple

	Principal Color
Nemophila menziesii baby-blue-eyes	Bright blue with white center
Phacelia campanularia California bluebell	Blue, occasionally white

 HERBACEOUS PERENNIALS

Armeria maritima var. *californica* thrift	Pink, white
Dicentra formosa western bleeding heart	Rose-purple to white
Dodecatheon hendersonii sailor caps	White to magenta

Species of the genus *Castilleja* (paintbrush) abound from coast to coast. Usually red, they occasionally sport yellow or orange flowers. This is *C. californica*, native to the West Coast.

Eriogonum arborescens wild buckwheat (shrub);	Pale pink to rose
also ***E. umbellatum*** var. ***polyantha*** and other wild buckwheats	Sulfur yellow
Heuchera 'Santa Ana Cardinal' coral-bells a hybrid of ***H. sanguinea*** and ***H. maxima***	Rose-red
Iris douglasiana, I. innominata, and hybrids between these two species California iris	Most plants sold are cultivars in white, cream, yellow, lavender, blue, reddish purple, or brown
Lewisia cotyledon no common name	White, tinged or striped red
Lilium pardalinum leopard lily	Crimson with lighter throat, spotted brown
Lupinus arboreus tree lupine	Yellow, occasionally lavender or blue
Romneya coulteri matilija poppy	White with golden stamens
Salvia clevelandii blue salvia (shrub)	Violet-blue
Salvia leucophylla gray or purple salvia	Light purple
Salvia sonomensis creeping salvia	Violet-blue
Sedum spathulifolium sedum	Light yellow
Sisyrinchium bellum blue-eyed grass	Purple to violet-blue
Trichostema lanatum wooly bluecurls	Blue

SHRUBS

Arctostaphylos densiflora 'Howard McMinn'; and ***A.densiflora*** 'Sentinel' both selections from the Sonoma manzanita	whitish pink

	Principal Color
Arctostaphylos edmundsii 'Carmel Sur' an evergreen ground cover selection from the Little Sur manzanita	Pink
Baccharis pilularis 'Twin Peaks' an evergreen ground cover selection from the dwarf coyote bush	Inconspicuous flowers
Ceanothus 'Julia Phelps' 'Concha' 'Dark Star' and others in ground-cover and upright forms California lilac	Cobalt blue Very dark blue Deep violet-blue
Dendromecon harfordii island tree poppy	Yellow
Fremontodendron californicum 'California Glory' flannel bush	Yellow, tinged red
Garrya elliptica 'James Roof' silk-tassel bush	Yellowish green catkins
Rhododendron occidentale western azalea	White to pinkish white
Ribes aureum golden currant	Bright yellow; red fruits turn black
Ribes sanguineum var. ***glutinosum*** red-flowered currant	Pink to red; blue-black fruit

---

Note: After having lived and gardened in California for twenty years, I can heartily endorse this list. Let me point out that some of the perennials and shrubs native to California's low-elevation habitats will not be winter-hardy in most other climates. Also, some plants strongly prefer the definite wet-dry weather cycles of California. The annuals perform well in most climates if they are grown on well-drained soil and are planted in early spring or early fall. In the wild, sizable plants develop during the winter rains and complete their bloom cycle before intensely dry weather arrives. Most annuals are not heat-resistant. Some of the species that grow in full sun in northern California are found in shaded canyons in the warmer, drier parts of southern California.

This cool-loving, low-growing California native annual, baby-blue-eyes, will produce color quickly from direct seeding in early spring or fall.

APPENDIXES
HARDINESS ZONE MAP
ACKNOWLEDGMENTS
PHOTO CREDITS
INDEX

How to Buy Seeds for Meadows

SEEDS FOR meadows are available in several formulations:

• Mixtures containing a major proportion of grass seeds and a minor proportion of mixed native and exotic flower seeds. Ounce for ounce of flower seeds, these are not good buys.

• Mixtures containing a major proportion of inert vermiculite filler and a minor proportion of mixed native and exotic flower seeds (less than an ounce in a pint). These are also of dubious value.

• Mixtures containing mixed seeds of native and exotic flowers with no grass seeds or inert fillers. Most seed mixtures for meadows are of this type and usually are formulated for specific geographical regions. These mixtures provide lots of quick color at relatively low cost per pound or ounce.

• Premium regional mixtures containing seeds of only native American wildflower species. These are the most expensive, and give better value if you start the seeds under protection and transplant the seedlings. Of these, mixtures containing mostly hardy perennials, with annuals serving as a "nurse crop," are the most desirable.

The reasons behind the composition of the first two kinds of mixtures are economic rather than horticultural. Grass seed and vermiculite are cheap; by using them, the marketer can fill a large can with a small amount of flower seeds. This lowers the cost to the mail-order or retail marketer but not to the ultimate buyer. You get little real value for your money.

In contrast, the reasons behind the mixture of native and exotic species with no filler are partly economic, partly horticultural. Some of the bright, high-germinating, quick-growing exotic annuals are prolific seeders and can be grown at relatively low cost per pound. Some of the native American annuals — chiefly western or southwestern species — are also relatively cheap to grow in irrigated western seed fields. The perennial native flowers are generally expensive to grow and usually germinate at relatively low, but acceptable, rates.

Because of these facts, premium mixtures of native American species are considerably more expensive than mixtures containing exotics. Some of the seeds are hand-collected from plentiful species in the wild rather than grown in western or Texan seed fields. The real value of such mixtures is not only in the long-lived meadows they can produce but also in the satisfaction of knowing that you are re-creating plant associations that might have grown in sunny clearings in your area in former times. (Some gardeners prefer to purchase seeds of individual native species rather than mixtures, which gives them better control over the proportion of each species in their meadow.)

How to Read the Analysis Labels of Seed Mixtures

SOME SEED companies label by botanical names, some by common names, and some by both. Most sell not only regional mixtures but special-purpose mixtures under creative names, evoking images of sunshine, country, children, fragrance, or other "hot buttons" known to produce sales. Some sell short-plant mixtures, blends of tall plants for cutting, mixtures of pastel colors or warm colors — anything your heart could desire.

Here are some of the species included in common mixtures for various parts of the country. U.S. natives are marked with an asterisk. The others are garden varieties developed from species native to other countries. "OTPK" means "only the packager knows"; a question mark means there is no way for a gardener to be sure.

Common Name	Botanical Name	Annual or Perennial
African daisy	*Dimorphotheca sinuata* and hybrids with *D. pluvialis*	Annual
Alyssum, sweet	*Lobularia maritima*	Annual
* Baby-blue-eyes	*Nemophila menziesii*	Perennial
Baby's breath, annual	*Gypsophila elegans*	Annual
Bachelor button	*Centaurea cyanus*	Annual
* Black-eyed Susan	*Rudbeckia hirta*	Perennial
* Blanketflower	*Gaillardia* × *grandiflora*	Perennial
Blue flax	*Linum perenne* and subspecies, or the native *L. lewisii*	Perennial
Bouncing bet	*Saponaria officinalis*	Perennial
* Buffalo eyes	*Nemophilia maculata*	Annual

* California bluebell	*Gilia capitata*	Annual
* California poppy	*Eschscholzia californica*	Perennial and annual in California
* California sunshine	*Lasthenia glabrata*	Annual
Catchfly, dwarf	*Silene armeria*	Annual
Chicory	*Cichorium intybus*	Perennial
* Chinese houses	*Collinsia heterophylla*	Annual
* Clarkia	Usually *Clarkia amoena*	Annual
Clover, crimson	*Trifolium incarnatum*	Annual
* Coneflower, clasping	*Dracopis amplexicaulis*	Annual
* Coneflower, purple prairie	*Echinacea purpurea*	Perennial
* Coreopsis, lance-leaved	*Coreopsis lanceolata* or *C. grandiflora*	Perennial
* Coreopsis, plains	*Coreopsis tinctoria*	Annual
Coreopsis, tickseed	See tickseed	
Cosmos, garden	*Cosmos bipinnatus*	Annual
Cosmos: red, yellow, and orange	*C. sulphureus*	Annual
Dame's rocket	*Hesperis matronalis*	Perennial
* Desert bluebells	*Phacelia campanularia?*	Annual
* Evening primrose	*Oenothera hookeri* or *O. biennis*	Perennial
Forget-me-not	*Myosotis sylvatica*	Annual
Foxglove	*Digitalis purpurea*	Perennial
* Gayfeather	Usually *Liatris pycnostachya* or *L. spicata*	Perennial
Globe amaranth	*Gomphrena globosa*	Annual
* Globe gilia	Probably *Gilia capitata*	Annual
* Gloriosa daisy	*Rudbeckia hirta* and triploid cultivars	Perennial and annual
* Indian blanket	*Gaillardia pulchella*	Annual
Larkspur	*Consolida ambigua*	Annual
* Lemon mint	*Monarda citriodora*	Perennial
* Lupine	Many *Lupinus* species	Perennial and annual
* Lupine, golden	*Lupinus densiflorus*	Perennial
* Lupine, sky blue	*Lupinus succulentus*	Perennial
* Mexican hat	*Ratibida columnifera*	Perennial

Common Name	Botanical Name	Annual or Perennial
* Missouri primrose	*Oenothera missouriensis (= O. macrocarpa)*	Perennial
* Mountain phlox (not a true phlox)	*Linanthus grandiflorus*	Annual
Ox-eye daisy	*Chrysanthemum leucanthemum*	Perennial
* Penstemon, showy	*Penstemon spectabilis*	Perennial
* Phlox, annual	*Phlox drummondii*	Annual
Pot marigold	*Calendula officinalis*	Annual
* Prickly poppy, white	*Argemone hispida* or *A. albiflora*	Perennial
Queen Anne's lace	*Daucus carota*	Perennial
Rattlesnake grass or quaking grass	*Briza minor*	Annual
* Rocky Mountain phlox	OTPK; perhaps *P. caespitosa*	Perennial
Rose mallow	*Lavatera trimestris*	Annual
Scarlet flax	*Linum grandiflorum rubrum*	Annual
Shasta daisy	*Chrysanthemum superbum*	Annual
Shirley or field poppy	*Papaver rhoeas*	Annual
Siberian wallflower	*Erysimum hieraciifolium (= Cheiranthus allionii)*	Annual
Statice	*Limonium sinuatum*?	Annual
Strawflower	*Helichrysum bracteatum*	Annual
* Sunflower	OTPK; *Helianthus* spp.	Perennial and annual
* Sunray	*Enceliopsis argophylla* or *E. covillei*	Perennial
* Sweet William, wild	*Phlox divaricata*, occasionally *P. maculata*, or *Silene armeria* (naturalized) (not to be confused with sweet William, *Dianthus barbatus*)	Perennial
Sword statice	OTPK; perhaps *Psylliostachys suworowii*	Annual
* Texas bluebonnet	*Lupinus subcarnosus*, but also applied to *L. texensis*	Annual
* Tickseed	*Bidens* spp.	Annual
* Tidy-tips	*Layia platyglossa*	Annual
Toadflax	One of many *Linaria* spp.; probably *L. maroccana* or *L. bipartita*	Annual
Yarrow or milfoil	*Achillea millefolium*	Perennial

Mail-Order Wildflower Seed and Plant Sources

THE FOLLOWING list is arranged by geographical regions, in order to help you find seed and/or plant producers of local species and ecotypes. You will find that many seed and plant producers offer species that are native to other geographical regions but that grow well for them. If you want to stick to species native to your own region, refer to the regional lists in Chapter 8.

Many mail-order wildflower nurseries charge from one to three dollars for their catalogues, but they will usually credit this amount against your first order. Because nurseries change their charges for catalogues frequently, I have made no attempt to list their cost. Most of the nurseries I wrote to responded that they propagate all plants

they sell, from seeds, divisions, or spores; this is noted in the listings. A few said they buy some of their plants from wholesalers and can't verify their sources. To the best of my knowledge, I have not listed nurseries that rely mostly or entirely on plants collected from the wild for their sales stock. Collecting from the wild has seriously depleted stands of many species in areas where collectors are concentrated. However, just because a nursery isn't listed here does not mean that it collects its stock from the wild. It simply isn't possible to find all the nurseries that sell wildflower seeds and plants. Furthermore, the inclusion of a nursery on this list does not imply a recommendation from either the author or the publisher. As far as we know, the companies listed are reputable, but each customer must decide whether the quality of the seeds and plants meets his or her expectations.

Northern United States and Eastern Canada

Conley's Garden Center
Boothbay Harbor, ME 04538
Plants of Maine wildflowers, ferns, and marsh plants

Mulligan Seeds
1600 Apeldoorn Ave.
Ottawa, Ontario
Canada K2C 1V5
Seeds of native Canadian wildflowers

Oakridge Nurseries
P.O. Box 182
East Kingston, NH 03872
Plants of native wildflowers and ferns

Otter Valley Native Plants
Box 31, RR 1
Eden, Ontario
Canada N0J 1H0
Nursery-propagated plants and seeds of native wildflowers

Putney Nursery, Inc.
Rt. 5
Putney, VT 05346
Seeds of wildflowers, alpines, and perennials; plants available to walk-in trade only

Wyrttun Ward
18 Beach St.
Middleboro, MA 02346
Plants of northeastern woodland wildflowers

Mid-Atlantic States

Amenity Plant Products
RD 5, Box 265
Mt. Pleasant, PA 15666
Nursery-propagated native plants, seeds of meadow species

Appalachian Wildflower Nursery
Rt. 1, Box 275A
Reedsville, PA 17084
All wildflower or woody native plants are propagated in the nursery or garden-grown at the nearby state college. Some are very local ecotypes; if a species is originally from afar, that is noted in the description.

Kurt Bluemel, Inc.
2543 Hess Rd.
Fallston, MD 21047
Nursery-propagated plants of wildflowers, ferns, and grasses, some natives

Natural Landscapes
354 North Jennerville Rd.
West Grove, PA 19390
Nursery-propagated plants of native wildflowers and woody plants

The Primrose Path
RD 2, Box 110
Scottdale, PA 15683
Choice selections from nursery-propagated native plants

Southeastern and Mid-Southern States

Arrowhead Nursery
Box 38, Watia Road
Bryson City, NC 28713
Nursery-propagated native plants

Boothe Hill Wildflower Seeds
23-B Boothe Hill
Chapel Hill, NC 27514
Seeds of wildflowers native to the southeastern United States

Brookside Wildflowers
Rt. 3, Box 740
Boone, NC 28607
All plants are nursery-propagated

Carolina Exotic Gardens
Rt. 5, Box 283A
Greenville, NC 27834
Greenhouse-propagated plants of carnivorous native species

Eco-Gardens
P.O. Box 1227
Decatur, GA 30031
Nursery-propagated plants of trilliums, hepaticas, and other native wildflowers, plus selections and hybrids

Flowerplace Plant Farm
P.O. Box 4865
Meridian, MS 39304
Nursery-propagated wildflowers, ferns, and grasses native to the Mississippi hills and coastal plain; some prairie species

Gardens of the Blue Ridge
P.O. Box 10
Pineola, NC 28662
Nursery-propagated native wildflowers, shrubs, and trees

Holbrook Farm
115 Lance Rd.
P.O. Box 368
Fletcher, NC 28732
Nursery-propagated cultivars of native wildflowers

Holland Wildflower Farm
290 O'Neal Lane
Elkins, AR 72727
Seeds of meadow mixtures and components, including several species native to the South

Jacob's Gardens
Rt. 2, Box 280
Troutman, NC 28166
Nursery-propagated plants of native wildflowers

Montrose Nursery
P.O. Box 957
Hillsborough, NC 27278
Nursery-propagated plants of native wildflowers; cultivars and species

Native Gardens
Rt. 1, Box 464
Greenback, TN 37742
Seeds and nursery-propagated plants of native wildflowers, grasses, and sedges; some species from other regions. Consultations available.

Native Nurseries
1661 Centerville Rd.
Tallahassee, FL 32308
Native wildflower seeds by mail; nursery-propagated plants of native north Florida plants available only to walk-in trade

Natural Gardens
4304 Shell Lane
Knoxville, TN 37918
Plants of native wildflowers

Niche Gardens
1111 Dawson Rd.
Chapel Hill, NC 27516
Nursery-propagated plants of native wildflowers and grasses; some adapted species from other regions

Ben Pace Nursery
Rt. 1, Box 925
Pine Mountain, GA 31822
Unusual species of wildflowers, shrubs, and trees, all nursery-propagated

Sunlight Gardens
Rt. 1, Box 600A
Andersonville, TN 37705
Nursery-propagated plants of native wildflowers, shrubs, and ferns

We-Du Nurseries
Rt. 5, Box 724
Marion, NC 28752
Nursery-propagated plants of native wildflowers, grasses, and ferns; many choice cultivars of wild species

Wildflower Nursery
1680 Highway 25–70
Marshall, NC 28753
Plants of native wildflowers, ferns, and shrubs

The Wildwood Flower
Rt. 3, Box 165
Pittsboro, NC 27312
Nursery-propagated native wildflowers and ferns

Woodlanders, Inc.
1128 Colleton Ave.
Aiken, SC 29801
Nursery-propagated plants of the southern Piedmont and coastal plain ecosystems: wildflowers, grasses, shrubs, vines, trees. Many species are hardy farther north.

Midwestern and Prairie States

Bluestem Prairie Nursery
Rt. 2, Box 92
Hillsboro, IL 62049
Nursery-propagated plants of native prairie and savanna ecosystems: wildflowers, grasses, and sedges. Seed mixtures for prairies contain only species native to Illinois.

Busse Gardens
Rt. 2, Box 238
Cokato, MN 55321
"We have twenty-three acres of virgin woods in which we grow colonies and plants under controlled conditions to produce divisions. We do not rape the woods. We increase Japanese painted fern by tissue culture. Our specialties are wildflowers and fern species for woodland and rock gardens."

Country Wetlands Nursery
P.O. Box 126
Muskego, WI 53150
Nursery-propagated plants of native wildflowers, grasses, sedges, and ferns for ponds, wetlands, and prairies. Seed mixtures are customized to the soil and water characteristics of each site.

Flowerland
P.O. Box 26
Wynot, NE 68792
Nursery-propagated plants of wildflowers and ferns

Gilberg Perennial Farms
2906 Ossenfort Rd.
Glencoe, MO 63038
Missouri ecotypes of prairie and woodland species, all nursery-propagated

Great Lakes Wildflowers
Box 1923
Milwaukee, WI 53201
Nursery-propagated plants of wildflowers and grasses native to the lower Midwest and prairies

Iowa Prairie Seed Company
110 Middle Rd.
Muscatine, IA 52761
Seeds of prairie wildflowers and grasses

Lafayette Home Nursery, Inc.
RR 1, Box 1A
Lafayette, IL 61449
*Long-established producer of seeds of prairie
wildflowers and grasses*

Landscape Alternatives, Inc.
1465 N. Pascal St.
St. Paul, MN 55108–2337
*Nursery-propagated plants of 150 species of
prairie wildflowers, ferns, and grasses. Starter
seeds were collected within a 100-mile radius of
the Twin Cities.*

Little Valley Farm
Rt. 3, Box 544
Spring Green, WI 53588
*Nursery-propagated plants and seeds of native
midwestern wildflowers and shrubs*

Midwest Wildflowers
Box 64
Rockton, IL 61072
Seeds of native wildflowers

Miller Grass Seed Co.
P.O. Box 81823
Lincoln, NE 68501
*Formerly in Hereford, Texas; seeds of native
wildflowers and grasses*

Missouri Wildflowers Nursery
9814 Pleasant Hill Rd.
Jefferson City, MO 65109
*Seeds and nursery-propagated plants of native
wildflowers and ferns; foundation plants and
seeds all from Missouri sources*

The Natural Garden
38W443 Highway 64
St. Charles, IL 60175
*Nursery-propagated plants of native midwestern
wildflowers; also meadow flower and prairie
grass seeds*

Prairie Moon Nursery
Rt. 3, Box 163
Winona, MN 55987
*Seeds and nursery-propagated plants of prairie
wildflowers, grasses, sedges, shrubs, and vines*

Prairie Nursery
P.O. Box 306
Westfield, WI 53964
*Plants of native midwestern wildflowers and
grasses propagated from seeds collected at the
nursery, and seeds of prairie species*

Prairie Restorations, Inc.
P.O. Box 327
Princeton, MN 55371
*Nursery-propagated plants of midwestern
grasses and wildflowers from seeds; contract
services in planning and planting*

Prairie Ridge Nursery/CRM Ecosystems, Inc.
RR 2, 9738 Overland Rd.
Mt. Horeb, WI 53572
*Nursery-propagated seeds and plants of native
midwestern grasses, sedges, and wildflowers for
prairies, wetlands, and woodlands; contract
services*

Prairie Seed Source
P.O. Box 83
North Lake, WI 53064
*Seeds of wildflowers and grass species native to
sand prairies, wet and mesic prairies, and oak
woods*

Purple Prairie Farm
RR 2, Box 176
Wyoming, IL 61491
Seeds of prairie wildflowers and cover grasses

Rice Creek Gardens, Inc.
11506 Highway 65
Blaine, MN 55434
*Nursery-propagated plants of native
wildflowers, ferns, and alpines, selected for
tolerance to extreme weather conditions*

Rocknoll Nursery
1639 Hess Rd.
Sardinia, OH 45171
"We are committed to nursery propagation of the plants we offer. On our farm we have twenty acres of woodland with several creeks and wet areas where we are continuing to naturalize foundation stock plants. We are working with the Botanical Gardens at the Cincinnati Zoo and the University of Cincinnati to tissue-culture endangered and protected natives. During the last two years they have cultured trilliums and other slow-growing species with some success."

Sharp Bros. Seed Co.
P.O. Box 140, Highway 4
Healy, KS 67850
Seeds of improved native grasses from ten states, grown in irrigated fields; also seeds of native wildflowers and shrubs

Stock Seed Farms, Inc.
Rt. 1, Box 112
Murdock, NE 68407
Seeds and nursery-propagated plants of native wildflowers and grasses

Wilderness Wildflower Division
Escaper, Inc.
P.O. Box 1664
Salina, KS 67402–1664
Seeds of native wildflowers from several regions

The Wildflower Source, Inc.
P.O. Box 312
Fox Lake, IL 60020
"Whenever possible we propagate native woodland flowers and ferns by division of established plants, which accounts for about 75 percent of our production."

Windrift Prairie Shop
RD 2
Oregon, IL 61061
Seeds of wildflowers and grasses

Southern Great Plains States

Antique Rose Emporium
Rt. 5, Box 143
Brenham, TX 77833
"We sell nursery-propagated plants and seeds of native Texas wildflowers in addition to old-timey roses."

Bamert Seed Co.
Rt. 3, Box 1120
Muleshoe, TX 79347
Seeds of native Texan and southern Great Plains grasses

Browning Seed, Inc.
Box 1836
Plainview, TX 78705
Seeds of native grasses and wildflowers

Cactus Farm
Rt. 5, Box 1610
Nacogdoches, TX 75961
Nursery-propagated plants of native cacti and succulents

Foster-Rambie Grass Seed
326 North Second St.
Uvalde, TX 78801
Seeds of native southwestern grasses

Green Horizons
218 Quinlan, Suite 571
Kerrville, TX 78028
Seeds of native southwestern wildflowers

J'Don Seeds International
P.O. Box 10998–533
Austin, TX 78766
Seeds of native southwestern wildflowers

Douglass W. King Co., Inc.
P.O. Box 20320
San Antonio, TX 78220–0320
Seeds of native Texas wildflowers and grasses

Lorany's Garden Center
11902 Alief-Clodine Rd.
Houston, TX 77082
Nursery-propagated plants of native southwestern wildflowers and grasses

The Lowrey Nursery
2323 Sleepy Hollow Rd.
Conroe, TX 77385
A pioneer producer of plants of species native to Texas, the Southwest, and northern Mexico; all nursery-propagated

Native American Seed
94 Jeter Rd.
Argyle, TX 76226
Seeds of native southwestern wildflowers and grasses

Neiman Environments Nursery
2701 Cross Timbers
Flower Mound, TX 75028
Nursery-propagated plants and seeds of native southwestern wildflowers and grasses

Robinson Seed Co.
1113 Jefferson Drive
Plainview, TX 79072
Seeds of native southwestern grasses

Turner Seed
Rt. 1, Box 292
Breckenridge, TX 76024
Seeds of native southwestern wildflowers and grasses

Rocky Mountain and Southwestern States

SOME SEED sources collect all over the West and northern Mexico. Also, considering the extent of cactus rustling in the Southwest and Mexico, it is important to ask about the origin of any cactus plant you purchase. Insist on nursery-propagated plants.

Absoroka Seed
Rt. 1, Box 97
Manderson, WY 82432
Seeds of native wildflowers

Bernardo Beach Native Plant Farms
No. 1 Sanchez Rd.
Veguita, NM 87062
"We mail-order seeds of southwestern native wildflowers species but do not sell plants by mail."

Curtis and Curtis Seed Co.
Star Rt., Box 8A
Clovis, NM 88101
Seeds of native grasses

Granite Seed
P.O. Box 177
Lehi, UT 84043
Seeds of meadow mixtures and components

Intermountain Cactus
2344 South Redwood Rd.
Salt Lake City, UT 84119
Nursery-propagated, winter-hardy cactus plants grown from cuttings or seeds; intermountain and northern Great Plains cactus species as well

Niels Lunceford, Inc.
Box 102
Dillon, CO 80435
Nursery-propagated plants of mountain wildflowers; also wildflower seeds

Mesa Garden
Box 72
Belen, NM 87002
Nursery-propagated plants and seeds of native cacti, succulent, and xerophytic species

Plants of the Southwest
Rt. 6, Box 11A
Aqua Fria Rd.
Santa Fe, NM 87501
Seeds and plants of native wildflowers, grasses, and American Indian vegetables; all plants nursery-propagated from seeds or divisions

Rocky Mountain Rare Plants
P.O. Box 20483
Denver, CO 80220–0483
Nursery-propagated plants and seeds of mountain wildflowers

Southwestern Native Seeds
P.O. Box 50503
Tucson, AZ 85703
"We gather small amounts of seeds from nonendangered native plants in the Southwest, Texas, and Mexico, mostly for collectors and botanical gardens."

Dean Swift Seed Company
P.O. Box B
Jaroso, CO 81138
Seeds of wildflowers

Wild and Crazy Seed Co.
P.O. Box 895
Durango, CO 81302
Nursery-propagated plants and seeds of mountain wildflowers and grasses

Wind River Seed
Rt. 1, Box 97
Manderson, WY 82432
Wholesale quantities of Wyoming native wildflowers, grasses, shrubs, and trees. "We harvest seeds of common flowers that occur in large stands, in years when they are abundant, but never in an amount that might damage the population. We don't collect seeds of rare plants."

Northwestern United States, Alaska, and Western Canada

Abundant Life Seed Foundation
P.O. Box 772
Port Townsend, WA 98368
Seeds of native northwestern plants

Fancy Fronds
1911 Fourth Ave. West
Seattle, WA 98119
Nursery-propagated fern plants

Forest Farm
990 Tetherow Rd.
Williams, OR 97544
Nursery-propagated plants of native North American wildflowers and woody species

Four Winds Nursery
5853 East Shore Rt.
Polson, MT 59860
Nursery-propagated plants of hardy northern plains and mountain species of wildflowers, grasses, and ferns; seeds of some species

Frosty Hollow Nursery
P.O. Box 53
Langley, WA 98260
Seeds of native northwestern wildflower, tree, shrub, and grass species for restoring native plant communities; planning services

Henry's Plant Farm
4522 132nd St. NE
Snohomish, WA 98290
Nursery-propagated plants of ferns, some native

High Altitude Gardens
P.O. Box 4619
Ketchum, ID 83340
Seeds of Idaho and native northwestern

wildflowers and grasses, including many species native to high-altitude habitats

Idaho Grimm Growers Warehouse Coop.
P.O. Box 276
Blackfoot, ID 83221
Seeds of native grasses

McLaughlin's Seeds
Buttercup's Acre
Mead, WA 99021–0550
Seeds of native northwestern wildflowers

Natural Legacy Seeds
RR 2, C1 Laird
Armstrong, British Columbia
Canada V0E 1B0
"We have one of the largest selections of ornamental grass seeds in North America and are strong in seeds of Canadian and northwestern U.S.A. wildflowers, especially penstemons. We carry seeds of some species from outside our bioregion."

Northplan/Mountain Seed
P.O. Box 9107
Moscow, ID 83843–1607
Seeds of many western species of wildflowers, grasses, shrubs, and trees for homes, range reclamation, and land restoration

Plants of the Wild
(Division of Seeds, Inc.)
P.O. Box 866
Tekoa, WA 99033
Nursery-propagated plants of native northwestern wildflowers

Siskiyou Rare Plant Nursery
2825 Cummings Rd.
Medford, OR 97501
Specializes in nursery-propagated plants of alpines and other dwarf, hardy wildflowers and fern species and in cultivars for woodland and rock gardens; some northwestern natives

Skyline Nursery
1654 Sequim-Dungeness Way
Sequim, WA 98382
Nursery-propagated plants of local species of wildflowers, grasses, trees, and shrubs

California and Nevada

Alpine Plants
P.O. Box 245
Tahoe Vista, CA 95732
Nursery-propagated plants native to western mountain areas

C. H. Baccus
900 Boynton Ave.
San Jose, CA 95117
Nursery-propagated plants of California wildflowers

California Flora Nursery
P.O. Box 3
Fulton, CA 95439
Nursery-propagated plants and seeds of native California wildflowers and grasses

Carter Seeds
475 Mar Vista Drive
Vista, CA 92083
Nursery-propagated plants and seeds of native California wildflowers and grasses

J. L. Hudson, Seedsman
P.O. Box 1058
Redwood City, CA 94064
Nursery-propagated plants and seeds of native California wildflowers and grasses

Larner Seeds
P.O. Box 407
Bolinas, CA 94924–0407
Seeds of native grasses and wildflowers in mixtures and separate species; nursery-propagated plants to walk-in trade only

Las Pilitas Nursery
Star Rt., Box 23X
Santa Margarita, CA 93453
Nursery-propagated plants of native California wildflowers, shrubs, and trees; also seeds of native wildflowers

Moon Mountain Wildflowers
P.O. Box 34
Morro Bay, CA 93443–0034
Seeds of native California wildflowers

Theodore Payne Foundation
10549 Tuxford St.
Sun Valley, CA 91352
Seeds and nursery-propagated plants of native California wildflowers and grasses. This organization has a long history of protecting native colonies of rare and endangered California wildflowers.

Redwood City Seed Company
Box 361
Redwood City, CA 94064
Seeds of native California wildflowers and grasses

S and S Seeds
P.O. Box 1275
Carpinteria, CA 93013
Seeds of meadow mixtures and components

Wildflower Seed Company
P.O. Box 406
St. Helena, CA 94574
Seeds of native California wildflowers

Wildwood Farm
10300 Sonoma Highway
Kenwood, CA 95452
Seeds and nursery-propagated plants of native California wildflowers and woody species and grasses

Sources for Meadow Seeds

Allen, Sterling and Lothrop
191 U.S. Rt. 1
Falmouth, ME 04105
Meadow seed mixtures

Applewood Seed Co., Inc.
P.O. Box 10761
Edgemont Station
Golden, CO 80401
Major producer of meadow seed mixtures and components (individual species)

W. Atlee Burpee Co.
300 Park Ave.
Warminster, PA 18974
"Our seeds of meadow mixtures are grown in cultivated fields, not gathered from the wild."

DeGiorgi Seed Company
6011 N Street
Omaha, NE 68117
Seeds of regional meadow mixes and components, and grasses

Environmental Seed Producers
P.O. Box 5904
El Monte, CA 91734
Principally wholesale; a major grower of seeds for meadow mixtures and components for commercial projects and roadside beautification

Johnny's Selected Seeds
310 Foss Hill Rd.
Albion, ME 04910
"We sell two regional meadow seed mixtures; the seeds are from cultivated crops rather than from the wild."

Park Seed Co.
Cokesbury Rd.
Greenwood, SC 29647–0001
Seeds of regional meadow mixtures, field-grown, not collected from wild colonies

Clyde Robin Seed Co.
P.O. Box 2366
Castro Valley, CA 94546
Major producer of seeds for meadow mixtures; 200 different wildflower and grass species. Free catalogue.

Vermont Wildflower Farm
Route 7
Charlotte, VT 05445
Specializes in regional meadow seed mixtures and components; ships all over North America. Seasonal display gardens.

Stokes Seeds
P.O. Box 548
Buffalo, NY 14240
Regional wildflowers, meadow seed mixtures, and components

Wildseed, Inc.
P.O. Box 308
Eagle Lake, TX 77434
"We are a major producer of wildflower seeds, mostly Texas, prairie, and western natives, and of seeds for meadow mixtures."

———

Special thanks are extended to the Clearinghouse of the National Wildflower Research Center; to Barbara Barton, author of *Gardening by Mail III*; and to the many state and regional wildflower societies for their help in compiling this list.

State, Regional, and National Wildflower Societies

Alabama Wildflower Society
240 Ivy Lane
Auburn, AL 36830

*Alaska Native Plant Society
P.O. Box 141613
Anchorage, AK 99514

Arizona Native Plant Society
P.O. Box 41206
Tucson, AZ 85717

Arkansas Native Plant Society
Department of Forest Resources
University of Arkansas at Monticello
Monticello, AR 71655

*California Native Plant Society
909 12th St., Suite 116
Sacramento, CA 95814

Canadian Prairie Lily Society
c/o A. D. Delahay
RR 5
Saskatoon, Saskatchewan
Canada S7K 3J8

*The Canadian Wildflower Society
75 Ternhill Crescent
North York, Ontario
Canada M1L 3H8

Colorado Native Plant Society
P.O. Box 200
Fort Collins, CO 80522

Idaho Native Plant Society
P.O. Box 9451
Boise, ID 83707

***Kansas Wildflower Society**
Mulvane Art Center, Washburn University
Topeka, KS 66611

Louisiana Native Plant Society
Rt. 1, Box 151
Saline, LA 71070

***Minnesota Native Plant Society**
220 Biological Science Center
1445 Gortner Ave.
St. Paul, MN 55108

***Mississippi Native Plant Society**
P.O. Box 2151
Starkville, MS 39759

Missouri Native Plant Society
P.O. Box 176
Department of Natural Resources
Jefferson City, MO 63102

Native Plant Society of New Mexico
443 Live Oak Loop N.E.
Albuquerque, NM 87122

Native Plant Society of Oregon
1920 Engel Ave. N.W.
Salem, OR 97304

***Native Plant Society of Texas**
P.O. Box 891
Georgetown, TX 78627

***New England Wild Flower Society**
(seeds of more than 200 species available)
Garden in the Woods
Hemenway Rd.
Framingham, MA 01701

New Jersey Native Plant Society
Frelinghuysen Arboretum
P.O. Box 1295 R
Morristown, NJ 07960

North American Wildflower Research Center
2600 FM 973 North
Austin, TX 78725

***North Carolina Wildflower Preservation Society**
900 West Nash St.
Wilson, NC 27893

***North Nevada Native Plant Society**
P.O. Box 8965
Reno, NV 89507

***Ohio Native Plant Society**
6 Louise Drive
Chagrin Falls, OH 44022

Pennsylvania Native Plant Society
1806 Commonwealth Building
316 Fourth Ave.
Pittsburgh, PA 15222

Society for Louisiana Irises
P.O. Box 40175
Lafayette, LA 70504

Society for Pacific Coast Native Iris
977 Meredith Court
Sonoma, CA 95476

Southern California Botanists
Department of Biology
Fullerton State University
Fullerton, CA 92634

Southern Illinois Native Plant Society
Botany Department
Southern Illinois University
Carbondale, IL 52901

Tennessee Native Plant Society
Department of Botany
University of Tennessee
Knoxville, TN 37996

*Utah Native Plant Society
3631 South Carolyn Street
Salt Lake City, UT 84106

Virginia Native Plant Society
P.O. Box 844
Annandale, VA 22003

Washington Native Plant Society
Department of Botany KB-15
University of Washington
Seattle, WA 98195

The Wild Ones — Natural Landscapers
Judi Ficks
10848 North Pebble Lane
Mequon, WI 53092

Wyoming Native Plant Society
P.O. Box 1471t
Cheyenne, WY 82003

Note: Some names and addresses are reproduced by permission from *Gardening by Mail III*, by Barbara Barton, published by Houghton Mifflin Company. Organizations that offer seed exchanges for members are marked with an asterisk. Inquire about sales to nonmembers; these can usually be arranged at a slightly higher price per packet. The New England Wild Flower Society publishes a frequently updated booklet, "Nursery Sources, Native Plants and Wildflowers," lists mail-order sources throughout the United States that propagate native herbaceous and woody plants. Inquire about the price.

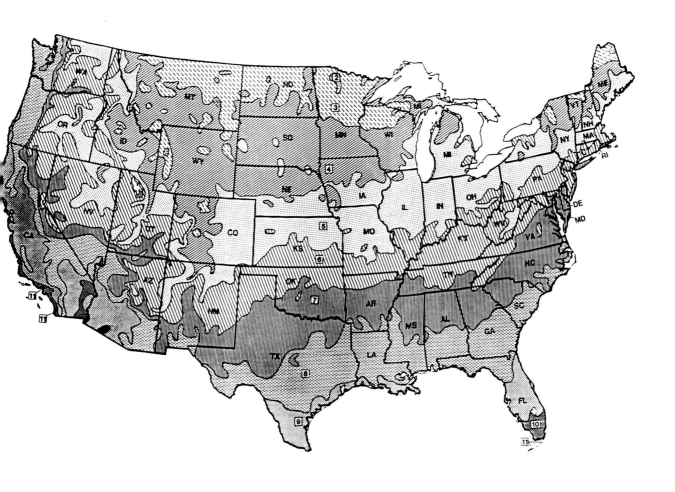

**Range of Average Annual Minimum
Temperatures for Each Zone**

ZONE 1	BELOW -50°F	
ZONE 2	-50° TO -40°	
ZONE 3	-40° TO -30°	
ZONE 4	-30° TO -20°	
ZONE 5	-20° TO -10°	
ZONE 6	-10° TO 0°	
ZONE 7	0° TO 10°	
ZONE 8	10° TO 20°	
ZONE 9	20° TO 30°	
ZONE 10	30° TO 40°	
ZONE 11	ABOVE 40°	

❧ ACKNOWLEDGMENTS

SPECIAL THANKS to my wife, Jane, and her botanizing friends in Texas, who introduced me to wildflowers: Chris Bayless, Dr. Charles D. Peterson, and Dr. Larry E. Brown; and to Dr. Steven R. Hill of the Clemson University Herbarium, who updated the nomenclature in this book and educates me on field trips to the Blue Ridge Mountains. The National Wildflower Research Center contributed a national overview on wildflowers.

For local and regional information on wildflowers, I thank Geyata Ajilvsgi, Bartlesville, Oklahoma; Nancy Arrington, Virginia Native Plant Society, Annandale, Virginia; Dr. Joseph L. "Leo" Collins of TVA's Natural Heritage Department, Knoxville, Tennessee; Dr. Michael N. Dana, Purdue University Department of Horticulture, Lafayette, Indiana; Doug and Cindy Gilberg, Gilberg Perennial Farms, Glencoe, Missouri; Gordon Hayward, landscape consultant, Westminster West, Vermont; Dr. A. R. Krukeberg, University of Washington, Seattle; Bob McCartney, Woodlanders, Inc., Aiken, South Carolina; Ken Moore, North Carolina Botanical Garden, Chapel Hill; Martha Oliver, the Primrose Path, Scottdale, Pennsylvania; Victor Rudis, Mississippi Native Plant Society, Starkville; Andrea Shea, Tennessee Department of Conservation; Dr. Erich Steiner, University of Michigan,

Ann Arbor; Sally Wasowski, landscape designer, and her husband, Andy, photographer, Dallas, Texas; and Dr. May Wright, Minnesota Native Plant Society, University of Minnesota, St. Paul.

For their advice on Chapter 2, "A Spring Garden in the Woods," I thank David E. Benner, New Hope, Pennsylvania; Barbara Emerson, garden writer, Chapel Hill, North Carolina; Judy Glattstein, landscape consultant, Wilton, Connecticut; Lynn Habig, Zionsville, Indiana; Paul James, Boones Mill, Virgina; Nell Lewis, Greensboro, North Carolina; Virginia Miller, Richmond, Virginia; Barbara Pryor of the New England Wild Flower Society, Framingham, Massachusetts; Libby Wilkes, Wayzata, Minnesota; and Hedi Wood, Townsend, Tennessee.

For help with Chapter 3, "Meadows," I thank Gail Barton and Richard Lowery, Flowerland, Meridian, Mississippi; Meredith Bradford-Clebsch and Dr. Ed Clebsch, Native Gardens, Greenback, Tennessee; Bruce and Kim Hawks, Niche Gardens, Chapel Hill, North Carolina; Donna Legare and Judy Walthal, Native Nurseries, Tallahassee, Florida; Dr. Robert E. Lyons, VPI & SU, Blacksburg, Virginia; Lucinda Mays, horticulturist, Callaway Gardens, Pine Mountain, Georgia; Betty Twiggs, landscape designer, Raleigh, North Carolina; and, for their special expertise in meadow flowers for highway landscaping, Dr. Will Corley, University of Georgia, Griffin, and Craig Steffens, landscape architect, Texas Highway Dept., Austin.

For their help with Chapter 4, "Prairies," I thank Barbara Anthony, Dallas-Fort Worth Airport, Texas; Brian Barker, Chicago Botanic Garden, Glencoe, Illinois; Adele P. Kleine, garden writer, Winnetka, Illinois; Dr. Virginia M. Kline, University of Wisconsin Arboretum, Madison; Lorrie Otto, the Wild Ones, Milwaukee, Wisconsin; Rachel Snyder, Kansas Native Plant Society, Mayetta; Guy Sternberg, landscape architect, Petersburg, Illinois; and Don Vorpahl, environmental landscape consultant, Hildreth, Wisconsin.

For their input on Chapter 5, "Western Wildflowers," I thank Robert Heapes, Parker, Colorado; Halli Mason, California Native Plant Society, and the Santa Monica Mountains Chapter of the CNPS; Ron Lutsko, Jr., landscape architect, San Francisco, California; Dean Olson, Lincoln City, Oregon; Dr. Jack Olson, Montana State University, Bozeman; Judith and Roland Phillips, Bernardo Beach Plant Farm, Veguita, New Mexico; Dr. Gerald R. Straley, University of British Columbia Botanical Garden, Vancouver; Mr. and Mrs. Tim Walker, Southwestern Native Seeds, Tucson, Arizona; and George Waters, editor, *Pacific Horticulture.*

For their help with Chapter 6, "Wildflowers for Damp or Wet Spots," I thank Dr. Edward L. Blake, Jr., Crosby Arboretum, Picayune, Mississippi; Ron Determann, horticulturist, Atlanta Botanical Garden, Georgia; Dr. Rob Gardner, University of North Carolina Botanical Garden, Chapel Hill; and Mildred Pinnell, horticulturist, Atlanta Botanical Garden.

For their help with Chapter 7, "Attracting Butterflies and Birds," I thank LuAnn Craighton, naturalist, Callaway Gardens, Pine Mountain, Georgia; Denise and Rob Gibbs, naturalists, Gaithersburg, Maryland; and Craig Tufts, National Wildlife Federation, Washington, D.C.

Last but not least, thanks to Ray Allen of Vermont Wildflower Farm, Charlotte, Vermont; Steve Atwood of Clyde Robin Seed Company, Hayward, California; John Bodger of Environmental Seed Producers, El Monte, California; Gene Milstein of Applewood Seed Co., Golden, Colorado; and John Thomas of Wildseed, Inc., Eagle Lake, Texas, for convincing me that mixtures of native and exotic wildflower seeds will be used for planting most meadows for some time to come.

PHOTO CREDITS

Robert Alexander, viii, 41, 51; Barbara Anthony, 180, 187; Gail Barton, 162; Chris Bayless, 101, 107, 199, 200; David Benner, frontispiece, 18–19, 31, 32–33; John Biever, 78–79, 80; Gerald Bishop, 132, 136; Ed Blake, 131; Everette Castoe, 35, 59, 159; W. L. Corley, 125; Michael H. Dodge (White Flower Farm), 27, 122; Barbara Emerson, 44–45, 46–47, 49, 142–43; Galen D. Gates, 87, 88, 89, 128; Denise Gibbs, 147, 150–51; Judy Glattstein, 24, 25, 37; Gordon Hayward, 20, 173; Robert Heapes, 108, 112–13; High Altitude Gardens, 115, 116–17; Paul James, 43, 154; Johnny's Selected Seeds, vi–vii, 84, 91, 203; Mary Ann Johnson, 14, 126–27; Kristi Jones, 206, 209; Virginia M. Kline, 75; Ron Lutsko, 96–97, 99; Robert Lyons, 38, 62, 63, 64, 65, 67; Judith Phillips, 103; Tom Pierson, 137; Clint Powers, 118, 189, 191; Kathy Rose, 52–53, 54, 55; Guy Sternberg, 72, 83; George Taloumis, 121, 139; Tim Walker, 102; Jane Griffith Wilson, 92, 104–5, 106; Jim Wilson, 2, 5, 6, 9, 10–11, 13, 42, 141, 166, 170, 177, 194; Frances Worthington, xi; Linda Yang, 71

INDEX

Dentaria laciniata (toothwort), 16
Deschampsia (tufted hairgrass), 176
Desmodium canadense (tick trefoil; beggar's lice) 179
Dicentra (bleeding heart), 143
Dicentra canadensis (squirrel corn), 156
Dicentra cucullaria (Dutchman's breeches), 156
Dicentra exemia (wild bleeding heart), *20, 31*
Dicentra formosa (western bleeding heart), 206
Dichromena latifolia (whitetop sedge), 130
Dodecatheon clevelandii (western shooting-star), 97
Dodecatheon hendersonii (sailor caps), 206
Dodecatheon meadia (shooting-star), 16, 77, 156, 166, 178, 188
Dogwood, 22, 82
Dracopis amplexicaulis (clasping-leaved coneflower), 196
Dragonhead: beautiful false, 201; false, 129, 186
Dropseed: northern, 183; prairie, 77
Drosera (sundew), 130
Dryopteris ludoviciana (Louisiana shield fern), 177
Dryopteris marginalis (marginal shield fern), 177
Dutchman's breeches, 156
Dutchman's pipe, 148
Dyssodia tenuiloba (bristle-leaf dyssodia), 196

E

Echinacea pallida (pale-purple coneflower), 179, 185
Echinacea paradoxa (golden coneflower), 185
Echinacea purpurea (purple or purple prairie coneflower), *viii, 41, 51, 78–79, 147*, 148, 166, 179, 185
Echinacea sanguinea (purple coneflower), 197
Elderberry, *139*
Elephantella, 115
Elephant-foot, 20, 166
Elephantopus nudatus (elephant-foot), 20
Elephantopus tomentosus (elephant-foot), 166
Elymus canadensis (nodding wild rye), 187
Epilobium angustifolium (fireweed), 116–17
Epilobium canum subspp. *angustifolium* (hummingbird flower), 96

Epilobium canum subspp. *garrettii* (orange zauschneria), 112
Epilobium canum subspp. *latifolium* (Arizona trumpet), 143
Erianthus alopecuroides (plume grass), *83*, 186
Erianthus giganteus (sugarcane plume grass), 176
Erigeron compositus (cutleaf daisy), 191
Erigeron pulchellus (robin's plantain), 166
Erigeron simplex (one-headed daisy), 192
Eriocaulon decangulare (hatpins), 130
Eriogonum (wild buckwheat), 146
Eriogonum annuum (wild buckwheat),193
Eriogonum arborescens (wild buckwheat), 207
Eriogonum fasciculatum (California buckwheat), 96
Eriogonum umbellatum (sulfur-flowered buckwheat), 115; var. *polyantha* (wild buckwheat), 207
Eriophyllum confertiflorum (golden yarrow), 96
Eryngium leavenworthii (eryngo), 198
Eryngium yuccifolium (rattlesnake-master), 72, 74, 75, 146, 180, 185
Eryngo, 198
Erythrina herbacea (coral bean), 167
Erythronium albidum (white dogtooth violet), 194
Erythronium americanum (yellow trout-lily), 16, 28, 156, 167
Erythronium grandiflorum (glacier lily), 116
Eschscholzia californica (California poppy), 67, 95–96, 115, 205
Eschscholzia mexicana (Mexican gold poppy), 196
Eupatorium, 12, *125*, 148
Eupatorium coelestinum (mistflower; hardy ageratum), *xi, 7, 55,* 167, 198
Eupatorium fistulosum (joe-pye weed), 7, *125*, 148, 167
Eupatorium rugosum (snow thoroughwort; white snakeroot), 36, 160
Eupatorium urticifolium. See *Eupatorium rugosum*
Euphorbia bicolor (snow-on-the-prairie), 194
Euphorbia corollata (flowering or tramp's spurge), 11, 167, 180
Euphorbia esula (leafy spurge), 190
Euphorbia marginata (snow-on-the-mountain), 194
Euphorbia pubentissima. See *Euphorbia corollata*

Eustoma grandiflorum (Texas bluebells), 198, *200*
Evening primrose, 5, 68, *104–5*, 143, 149; Engelmann's, 195; Mexican, 203; showy, *59*, 171; white-tufted, *103*, 109, 202
Evening snow, 205

F

Fairy-wand, 165
Featherfleece, 129
Fern(s), 28, 29, 36, *126–27*, 177; American maidenhair, 177; Christmas, 29, 177; cinnamon, 177; creeping, 130; interrupted, 177; Louisiana shield, 177; maidenhair, 29, 177; marginal shield, 177; netted chain, 177; New York, 177; royal, 177; southern lady, 177; southern shield, 177
Fetterbush, 21; mountain, 21
Feverfew, American, 171, 181
Filipendula rubra (queen-of-the-prairie), 129, 160
Fire pink, 16, 174
Firethorn, 152
Fireweed, 116–17
Firewheel, 167
Flannel bush, 208
Flax: blue, 202; stiff-stem, 196
Floating heart, 130
Foamflower, 16, 17, *35*, 157, 175
Fothergilla gardenii (fothergilla), 22
Four o'clock, 100
Fremontodendron californicum 'California Glory' (flannel bush), 208
Fried-egg plant, 95
Fringe tree, 22

G

Gaillardia, 149; fragrant, 196; red, 197
Gaillardia amblyodon (red gaillardia), 197
Gaillardia aristata (blanketflower), *44–45, 55*, 202
Gaillardia pulchella (Indian blanket; firewheel), 67, 167, 197
Gaillardia suavis (fragrant gaillardia), 197
Galax aphylla. See *Galax urceolata*
Galax urceolata (galax), 17, 156
Garrya elliptica 'James Roof' (silk-tassel bush), 208
Gaultheria hispidula (creeping snowberry), 129
Gaultheria procumbens (wintergreen; teaberry), 129, 167
Gaura coccinea (scarlet gaura), 197
Gaura lindheimerii (white gaura), 194, *194*

Ruellia humilis (wild petunia), 182
Ruellia nudiflora (violet ruellia), 201
Rush, 176
Rye, nodding wild, 187

S
Sage, 143; autumn, 144, 204; blue, 201, 204; cherry, 204; lyre-leaved, 174; mealycup, 9; pitcher, 204; scarlet, 144, 174; tropical, *xi*, 5, 8, 142, 143, 198
Sagittaria (arrowhead), 130
Sailor caps, 206
St. Johnswort, 160, 168
Salvia, 143–44; blue, 201, 207; creeping, 207; gray or purple, 207
Salvia azurea var. *grandiflora* (blue or pitcher sage), 201, 204
Salvia clevelandii (blue salvia), 207
Salvia coccinea (scarlet or tropical sage), *xi*, 5, 142, 143, 174, 198
Salvia farinacea (mealycup sage; blue salvia), 9, 201
Salvia greggii (autumn or cherry sage), 144, 204
Salvia leucophylla (gray or purple salvia), 207
Salvia lyrata (lyre-leaved sage), 174
Salvia sonomensis (creeping salvia), 207
Salvia splendens (scarlet sage), 144
Sanguinaria canadensis (bloodroot), *24*, 157, 174, 188
Sapium sebiferum (Chinese tallow or popcorn tree), 127
Sarracenia (pitcher plant), 130
Satureja georgiana. See *Calamintha georgiana*
Saururus cernuus (lizard's-tail), 28, 130
Savory, Georgia, 165
Scarlet pea, 197
Schizachyrium scoparium (little bluestem), 183, 187
Scutellaria drummondii (skullcap), 201
Scutellaria integrifolia (narrow-leaved skullcap), 174
Sedge(s), 176; evergreen, 176; Fraser's, 176; whitetop, 130
Sedum spathulifolium (sedum), 207
Sedum ternatum (stonecrop), 174
Senecio aureus (golden ragwort), 161
Senna, 185; prairie, 188; wild, 160
Serviceberry, 152
Shinleaf, 172
Shooting-star, 16, 77, 156, 166, 178, 188; western, 97
Shortia galacifolia (shortia; Oconee bells), 17, 35, 174
Shrubs, 82, 207–8

Siberian bugloss, *24*
Side-oats grama, 183, 187
Silene polypetala (fringed catchfly), 174
Silene virginica (fire pink), 16, 174
Silk-grass, 168
Silk-tassel bush, 208
Silphium, 74
Silphium dentatum, 9, 174; var. *gatesii*, 174
Silphium integrifolium (rosinweed), 182
Silphium laciniatum (compass plant), *75*, 182, 186
Silphium perfoliatum (cup plant), 152, 186
Silphium terebinthinaceum (prairie dock), *75*, 152, 182, 186
Sine acaulis (moss campion), 192
Sisyrinchium atlanticum (blue-eyed grass), 6, 174
Sisyrinchium bellum (blue-eyed grass), 207
Sisyrinchium macrocarpum (yellow-eyed grass), 192
Sisyrinchium montana (blue-eyed grass), 192
Sisyrinchium pruinosum (dotted blue-eyed grass), 201
Skullcap, 201; narrow-leaved, 174
Skunk cabbage, 130
Smilacina racemosa (false Solomon's seal), 117, 174
Smilax herbacea (smilax), 175
Snakehead, 165
Snakeroot, white, 36
Sneezeweed, 167
Snowberry, creeping, 129
Snow-on-the-mountain, 194
Snow-on-the-prairie, 194
Snow thoroughwort, 160
Solidago, 6, 175, 184
Solidago caesia (blue-stemmed goldenrod), 175
Solidago curtisii, 175
Solidago flexicaulis (zigzag goldenrod), 161
Solidago odora (sweet goldenrod), 175
Solidago petiolaris (downy goldenrod), 196
Solidago speciosa (showy goldenrod), 183
Solidago sphacelata (false goldenrod), 175
Solidago stricta (slim goldenrod), 175
Solomon's-seal, 172; false, 117, 174; great, 157, 195
Sorbus (mountain ash), 152
Sorghastrum nutans (Indiangrass), *150–51*, 183, 187
Sorrel: redwood, 116; violet wood, 17, 200

Sourwood, 22
Spartina pectinata (cordgrass), 77
Sphaeralcea angustifolia (copper mallow), 196
Sphaeralcea coccinea (scarlet globemallow), 107, 204
Spider-lily, 130
Spiderwort, 182; common, 175; hairy-stemmed, 175; Ohio, 201; prairie, 201; zigzag, 175
Spigelia marilandica (Indian pink), 142, 175
Spiranthes (ladies' tresses), 171
Spleenwort, ebony, 29, 177
Sporobolus (prairie dropseed), 77
Sporobolus heterolepis (northern dropseed), 183
Spring beauty, 12, 165, 193
Spurge: Allegheny, 17, *166*; flowering, 11, 167, 180; Japanese, 17; leafy, 190; tramp's, 180
Squirrel corn, 156
Stachys drummondii (pink mint), 198
Staphylea trifolia (bladdernut), 82
Starflower, 158, *189*
Stargrass, yellow, 160, 169
Stellaria pubera (giant chickweed), 177
Stenanthium gramineum (featherfleece), 129
Stokesia laevis (Stokes' aster), 148, *162*, 175
Stonecrop, 174
Sumac, fragrant, 82
Sundew, 130
Sundrops, 9, 11–12, *162*, 171, 181
Sunflower, 7, 71, 149, 152, *187*; ashy, 167; false, 180; giant, 152; Maximilian, 152, 167; Mexican, 135; narrow-leaved, 167; rough, 167; silver, 9; swamp, 196; tickseed-, 152, 164
Swamp pink, 130
Sweet everlasting, 6, 167
Sweet flag, 130
Sweet William, wild, 172
Switchgrass, 76, 183

T
Teaberry, 167
Tephrosia onbrychoides (multibloom tephorsia), 195
Texas paintbrush, 197
Texas plume, 142, 143, 169, 197
Thalictrum polygamum. See *Thalictrum pubescens*
Thalictrum pubescens (tall meadow-rue), 161
Thelesperma filifolium (green thread), 196
Thelypteris kunthii (southern shield fern), 177